INCORPORATION AND BUSINESS GUIDE
FOR ALBERTA

INCORPORATION AND BUSINESS GUIDE
FOR ALBERTA

Tom Carter, LLB

Self-Counsel Press
(a division of)
International Self-Counsel Press Ltd.
Canada   USA

Self-Counsel Press acknowledges the financial support of the Government of Canada through the Book Publishing Industry Development Program (BPIDP) for our publishing activities.

Printed in Canada.

First edition: 2001

Canadian Cataloguing in Publication Data
Carter, Tom (G. Thomas), 1950
   Incorporation and Business Guide for Alberta

   (Self-counsel legal series)
   ISBN 1-55180-356-9

   1. Incorporation — Alberta — Popular works. 2. Private companies — Alberta — Popular works   I. Title.   II. Series
KEA316.Z82C37 2001   346.7123'06622   C2001-911443-5
KF1420.29C37 2001

Self-Counsel Press
(a division of)
International Self-Counsel Press Ltd.

1481 Charlotte Road	1704 N. State Street
North Vancouver, BC V7J 1H1	Bellingham, WA 98225
Canada	USA

CONTENTS

SAMPLES

INCORPORATION SERVICES AVAILABLE FROM THE PUBLISHER

To incorporate your company, you will need to file certain forms. You may type these yourself, but it is easier and quicker to use preprinted forms; or, if you wish, you can take advantage of our typing service and have all the forms typed out for you. Note: If you use the typing service, you do not need to purchase the preprinted forms.

Typing service

If you have decided to incorporate in Alberta, why not use Self-Counsel's convenient typing service and have all the forms typed out for you? The service covers the cost of the preprinted forms and the typing out of these forms according to information that you provide. We do not file the documents for you, nor does the typing service fee cover your filing fees.

Cost: $125 plus GST

If you have decided to incorporate a small, non-distributing company, here's how we can help you:

1. Read this book carefully before contacting us. Call (604) 986-3366 or 1-800-663-3007 between 8:30 a.m. and 5:00 p.m. and we will mail or fax the data sheets to you. Or download the data sheets from our Web site at <www.self-counsel.com>.

2. Reserve the name you have chosen with the Registrar of Companies.

3. Use the *Incorporation and Business Guide* as a reference to complete the data sheets, and then mail, fax, or e-mail the sheets back to us, together with your cheque, money order, or MasterCard/Visa number.

Mail to: Self-Counsel Press   Fax to: (604) 986-3947
           1481 Charlotte Road   E-mail to: incorp@self-counsel.com
           North Vancouver, BC V7J 1H1

4. When we receive your data sheets, we will type up the documents and return them to you for filing with the Registrar of Companies.

Please note that while your documents will be completed by competent personnel, we cannot and do not give legal advice. If you have complicated tax or legal problems with incorporation, you should see a lawyer.

Preprinted forms

Self-Counsel's preprinted *Incorporation Forms and Disk* kit contains copies of the forms you will need for a simple incorporation in Alberta. The kit contains:

- 2 copies of the Articles of Incorporation
- 2 copies of the Notice of Address or Notice of Change of Address
- 2 notices of the Notice of Directors or Notice of Change of Directors
- 1 copy of By-laws
- 2 copies of the Register of Directors
- 2 copies of the Register of Shareholders (Members)
- 2 copies of the Minutes of Annual General Meeting of Shareholders
- 2 copies of the Minutes of Annual General Meeting of Directors
- 4 share certificates

Along with the preprinted forms, the kit also includes a PC 3½" disk that contains electronic versions of the forms in Word 6.0 and PDF format.

The forms are designed to be used in conjunction with this book. Read them carefully and complete them by following the instructions and samples in this book.

Cost: $23.95

If you are unable to purchase the forms at the store where you purchased this book, complete and mail the order form.

✂ - ✄

ORDER FORM

Please send me the following items prepaid:

Item	Quantity	Unit Price	Total
Incorporation Forms for Alberta	_____	$23.95	_____
Minute book*	_____	$22.95	_____
Extra share certificates*	_____	$ 0.50 each	_____

SEALS AND STAMPS

Seals and stamps are not shipped from Self-Counsel Press. They are shipped directly from the manufacturer.

Seal, up to 39 characters (include spaces)*	_____	$45.95	_____
Seal, 40 or more characters (include spaces)*	_____	$55.95	_____
Deposit stamp (with 2 lines)*	_____	$16.95	_____
Endorsement stamp*	_____	$12.95	_____
Name and address stamp (with 3 lines)*	_____	$16.95	_____
Subtotal			_____
***Add PST to items marked with ***			_____
Add 7% GST calculated on Subtotal			_____
Postage & handling books, kits, etc. (includes GST)		$3.50	_____
Postage & handling seals & stamps (includes GST)		$5.00	_____
TOTAL			_____

All prices subject to change without notice.

Please send the items checked above to:

Mr./Ms._____

Address _____City _____

Province_____Postal code _____Telephone _____

Name of corporation_____

Corporation address (for stamp) if not same as above _____

Please charge my   ❏ Visa   ❏ MasterCard

MasterCard/Visa number _____

Expiry date _____

Signature _____

Please check your seals and stamps upon receipt.
We will not be responsible for errors reported more than 30 days after mailing.

NOTICE

1
BEFORE YOU INCORPORATE: WHAT YOU NEED TO KNOW

When I was practising law, I was surprised at the number of people who wanted to run their own businesses but assumed they couldn't do that unless they incorporated a company. They didn't understand that there are several legitimate ways to carry on a business. While incorporation is the right choice for many, it is not the right choice for all.

Before you plunge into incorporation, I want you to be sure it is the right choice for you. That's why I begin this book with a discussion of the three different ways of carrying on a private business.

1. Do You Really Need to Incorporate?

There are three ways to carry on business, and it is important for you to know the advantages and disadvantages of each. Once you understand each way, you will be equipped to decide if it's really necessary for you to incorporate.

1.1 Sole proprietorship

A sole proprietorship is an unincorporated business that you own and operate by yourself. But even though sole proprietorships are simply one-person operations, there are thousands of them, and they carry on an incredible variety of business activities. Most home-based businesses are unincorporated sole proprietorships, and almost every incorporated business started out as the unincorporated gleam in its founder's eye.

There are many advantages to sole proprietorship. One of the biggest of these is control. For example, as a professional writer, I am sole proprietor of my unincorporated writing business. I do all the work myself — make contacts with editors and publishers, discuss ideas for projects, negotiate the contracts, do the research, write the material, send it in, send in my bill — all in my own name. Like other writers, I am free to hire someone to help me if I wish. If I needed to do so, I could hire a researcher to dig up information for me or a typist to re-do a manuscript, but that doesn't change the fact that I own and operate my business.

All the income I earn from my business is mine. I don't have a separate bank account for my business earnings, because I don't need one, but I do keep track of what I earn from my business as I must report that income on my tax return every year. However, like any sole proprietor, I am free to deduct from that income any and all legitimate expenses of carrying on my business. This is an important point that many people misunderstand. *You don't have to incorporate to deduct business expenses.*

Many people also think they must incorporate to protect the name they use to carry on business, but this is not so. Anyone operating a sole proprietorship can take steps to ensure that their business name is protected. For example, let's say that Sally Smith has her own, sole-proprietorship business making custom-designed tablecloths. She calls her business Sally's Table Trappings. This is called a trade name, and it is perfectly legal for Sally to use it, provided it is not already in use by someone else. If Sally wants to be sure that no one else is using this name, she can order a search of all similar trade names currently registered with Alberta Corporate Registry by going to any private registry office.

As her business grows and her trade name becomes known, Sally might worry that someone might take advantage of it, either by using it outright or by using a close variation of it that might confuse her customers. If she hasn't done so already, she can protect herself by registering her trade name at Corporate Registry by filing a Declaration of Trade Name. (See Sample 1.) She can do this through any private registry office. Sally would simply fill out the form, take it to any one of the private registry services in Alberta, and pay the necessary fees. Alberta Corporate Registry charges $10 to register a Declaration of Trade Name, and each private registry office charges its own fee on top of that.

(Incidentally, this example illustrates another of the advantages of operating as a sole proprietor: aside from the Declaration of Trade Name,

Declaration of Trade Name

Partnership Act

I, SALLY SMITH
Name of Declarant

of 12345 67 AVE. EDMONTON AB A1B 2C3
Resident Address in Full

declare that:

1. I have been carrying on or intend to carry on the business of

   manufacture and sale of table linens.
   Type of Business

   in EDMONTON , in the Province of Alberta, under
   City, Town, Village

   the name of SALLY'S TABLE TRAPPINGS
   Trade / Business Name

   Use of this name commenced on 1 JAN 2000
   Day / Month / Year

2. No other person or persons are associated in partnership with me in

   this business.

SALLY SMITH
Name of Declarant (please print)

1 JAN 2000
Date of Declaration

BUSINESS PERSON
Occupation

[DRIVER'S LICENSE #]
Identification

This information is being collected for the purposes of corporate registry records in accordance with the Partnership Act. Questions about the collection of this information can be directed to the Freedom of Information and Protection of Privacy Coordinator for Alberta Registries, Research and Program Support, 3rd Floor, Commerce Place, 10155 - 102 Street, Edmonton, Alberta T5J 4L4, (780) 422-7330.

REG 3018 (99/01)

which is optional but highly recommended, there are no papers to file with the Alberta government. You can just get started.)

Of course, there are disadvantages to sole proprietorships. One of these is that the law does not perceive the sole proprietor and his or her business as separate entities; the proprietor and his or her business are considered one and the same. That means that Sally is *personally* responsible for the costs she incurs while operating her business. If she bought some supplies for her business, such as expensive cloth or a new sewing machine, and hadn't made enough money that month to pay for them, she would have to dip into her private funds to cover the bill. If she didn't pay, she would be sued personally, and if she lost, she would have to pay the judgement out of her own pocket. In other words, she personally faces unlimited liability for the debts of her business.

However, if Sally incorporates her business, her corporation would be the buyer of these items. If her corporation couldn't pay, it would be sued, not Sally herself. Any court judgement could be satisfied only out of the corporation's funds, and Sally's own money would not be at risk, owing to a combination of two features of incorporated companies: separate legal entity and limited liability. (For a further discussion of these characteristics, see sections **1.3a** and **1.3c**.)

One other disadvantage of sole proprietorship is that when the sole proprietor dies, the proprietorship dies. In the case of Sally's Table Trappings, any equipment and assets that Sally had used to run the business would pass under her will to the beneficiaries of her estate to be disposed of as they wish. (This is one way in which a sole proprietorship differs from an incorporated business, which does not die with its owner. An incorporated business continues to exist, a feature called perpetual existence, and ownership of the company can be easily transferred, as we shall see in section **2.2**.)

Of course, as a sole proprietor, Sally is free to try to sell her business at any time before she dies, if she can find an interested buyer who isn't afraid that her customers will go elsewhere. Customers often feel a close bond with the sole proprietor, and they may not be willing to continue to do business with a new owner whom they don't know and with whom they have never dealt, especially if there are many other businesses offering the same products or services.

1.2 Partnerships

The second common way of carrying on business without incorporating is by forming a partnership. Unlike sole proprietorships, which are not covered by any specific piece of legislation, partnerships in Alberta are governed by the Partnership Act, which gives us definitions of three important terms:

- *Partnership:* The relationship that subsists between persons carrying on a business in common with a view to profit. [As you would expect, this definition confirms that a partnership involves more than one person, but it doesn't say how many a partnership may involve. In fact, you can have two partners, 22, or more.]

- *Business:* Business includes every trade, occupation, and profession, so partnerships can carry on almost any type of business you can imagine.

- *Firm* and *firm name:* Persons who have entered into a partnership with one another are collectively called a firm, and the name under which their business is conducted is called a firm name. A partnership can protect its firm name by filing a Declaration of Trade Name, if it wishes.

Partnerships are commonly used by lawyers, accountants, and other professionals, but they can also be used by people who do not wish to incur the cost and complexity of incorporating.

Let's assume that Sally has talked about her idea for a custom table-decoration business with her friend and next-door neighbour, Mary, who thinks it is a great idea. Sally has the sewing and design experience, and Mary knows lots of people who entertain lavishly and would be willing to pay for unique, exotic tablecloths and napkins. The pair decide to start the business together. Because there are two of them, their business can't be a sole proprietorship. And they don't want to go through all the formalities and expense of incorporation, because they aren't sure yet if the business will succeed.

In fact, Sally and Mary will be partners, and unless they decide to write their own partnership agreement, their business relationship will be governed by some basic rules found in the Alberta Partnership Act. The most important of these is that each partner is an agent of the firm and of the other partners. This means that each is personally liable for the actions of the others due to a legal principle called *joint and several liability.* For example, Sally might decide to order some expensive gold thread or a fancy sewing machine. Even if Mary knows nothing about this, the principle of joint and several liability means that Mary will still be personally responsible for payment of the bill.

Because of this principle, Sally and Mary had better be sure they trust one another, since each has the power to expose the other to significant liability. However, the news is not all bad. There is another principle that says *all the partners are entitled to share equally in the capital and profits of the business.* So if Sally and Mary make money, they share it equally, unless, of course, they have a written agreement stating otherwise. A partnership does not file its own tax return, but it does have to keep track of its income and expenses, and Sally and Mary must report their shares of any profits as income on their personal tax returns every year. Sally and Mary will prepare a financial statement for the partnership each year showing how they divided the profits.

While partnerships that deliver professional services do not have to file any documents at Corporate Registry, partnerships that engage in manufacturing, trading, contracting, or mining do. Specifically, such partnerships must file a Declaration of Partnership, which must be signed by all the partners. It must give the partners' names, occupations, and residences; set out the name of their firm; state how long the firm has existed and will exist; and confirm that they are all the partners involved in it.

A sample of the Declaration of Partnership that Mary and Sally will file is included here. (See Sample 2.) The Corporate Registry fee for filing it is $10, and the private registries charge their own fee on top of that.

The Partnership Act sets out many other rules for partnerships. Some of these concern the retirement of partners and the addition of new partners. Since a partnership does not necessarily survive the death of a partner, there are also rules for winding it down if a partner dies. Again, if Sally and Mary do not want these rules to apply to their partnership, they would have to create their own partnership agreement that sets out the arrangements they prefer.

The Partnership Act also provides rules for a special kind of partnership called a limited liability partnership. As the name suggests, such partnerships exist to soften the impact of unlimited liability on partners. In a limited liability partnership, liability rests on the shoulders of a general partner. Liability of the other partners is limited to their stake in the partnership. Limited liability partnerships are never used by new businesses of the kind we are discussing, so details of these partnerships are not discussed in this book. For a further discussion of limited liability partnerships and also of partnership agreements, see *The Canadian Legal Guide for Small Business,* available from Self-Counsel Press.

SAMPLE 2
DECLARATION OF PARTNERSHIP

Declaration of Partnership

Partnership Act

We, _____ SALLY SMITH _____
Name of Declarant

_____ MARY JONES _____
Name of Declarant

declare that:

1. We are carrying on or intend to carry on the business of

    _____ manufacture and sale of table linens _____
    Type of Business

    in _____ EDMONTON _____, in the Province of Alberta, under the name
    City, Town, Village

    of _____ SALLY & MARY'S TABLE TRAPPINGS _____
    Business Name

2. The said partnership has existed since _____ 1 JUNE 2000 _____, and that the
    Day / Month / Year

    partnership will exist;   (a) ☐ until _____
    Day / Month / Year

             (b) ☑ for an indefinite period.

3. The persons named in the declaration are the sole members of the partnership.

4. Date of declaration _____ 2 JUNE 2000 _____
    Day / Month / Year

5. Name, Address, Occupation and Identification of Partners *(If more than two partners, please attach a list)*

    Name: ____ SALLY SMITH ____

    Resident Address: ____ 12345 67 AVE. _____ EDMONTON ____ AB ____ A1B 2C3
                                                   City, Town, Village   *Province*   *Postal Code*

    Occupation: ____ BUSINESS PERSON ____

                                             [DRIVER'S LICENSE#]
                                                Identification

    Name: ____ MARY JONES ____

    Resident Address: ____ 12347 67 AVE. _____ EDMONTON ____ AB ____ A1B 2C3
                                                   City, Town, Village   *Province*   *Postal Code*

    Occupation: ____ BUSINESS PERSON ____

                                             [DRIVER'S LICENSE#]
                                                Identification

This information is being collected for the purposes of corporate registry records in accordance with the Partnership Act. Questions about the collection of this information can be directed to the Freedom of Information and Protection of Privacy Coordinator for Alberta Registries, Research and Program Support, 3rd Floor, Commerce Place, 10155 - 102 Street, Edmonton, Alberta T5J 4L4, (780) 422-7330.

REG 3097 (99/01)

1.3 Corporation

The third way to carry on business is through an incorporated company, also called a limited liability corporation, or just simply a corporation. Corporations are distinct from sole proprietorships and partnerships because of three special legal principles that apply only to corporations, and not to sole proprietorships or partnerships. These principles are separate legal entity, perpetual existence, and limited liability. You must understand each of these before you can understand the advantages and disadvantages of incorporating.

1.3a Separate legal entity

When it comes to corporations, the law plays a game of "let's pretend." The law pretends that a properly constituted corporation is an independent personality, separate and distinct from its incorporators.

This bears repeating: a corporation is recognized by the law as something altogether different and apart from the human beings who create it. It is every bit as real as they are as far as the law is concerned. This is so even though a corporation can't do anything by itself. It has to have human beings to make it work.

The concept of separate legal entity is one of the great leaps of the legal imagination; perhaps the greatest, if you consider that without it, the world of modern business, with its giant multinational corporations, could not exist.

1.3b Perpetual existence

A corollary of separate legal identity is that a corporation has the potential to exist forever. The people who set it up will die, but that has no effect on the corporation. It will continue to exist as long as it is kept up to date with Alberta Corporate Registry, or until it is closed down by those who control it.

1.3c Limited liability

The third principle relates to the need to give entrepreneurs protection from the costs of taking on new and potentially risky business ventures. As we have seen, sole proprietors and partners are fully liable for the costs they incur while doing business. If the business doesn't have the money to pay, they are personally responsible for the entire amount. However, by creating the corporation — this new legal creature with separate identity and perpetual existence — those behind the corporation are sheltered by the law. Only the corporation is responsible for its business debts, and it can pay those only out of its own assets. The people who stand behind the corporation are not personally responsible to pay its bills if it can't.

This may sound like a recipe for fraud. All kinds of legitimate bills could be avoided if people set up corporations to do their business for them and put little or no money into those corporations. However, in the real world, very little business is done with corporations that aren't seen as creditworthy. If the person doing business with a corporation has any doubts about its ability to pay, he or she will look for additional guarantees of payment. The most common of these is a personal guarantee from the owners of the corporation. This document, signed by the owners of the corporation, makes them fully liable for the costs incurred if the corporation is unable to pay. For more information on personal guarantees, see section **2.1b**.

These three principles are at the foundation of any corporation, whether it be a one- or two-person business or a giant like General Motors. Together, they are the reason why the corporate form has become the preferred way of doing business in our economy. Now that we understand them, let's take a look at the advantages of using a corporation for business, from the point of view of our two entrepreneurs, Sally and Mary, and look at some other factors they need to consider as they think about setting up their own corporation.

2. Seven Factors to Consider before Incorporating

2.1 The limits of limited liability

Limited liability is the main thing many people think about when they start a corporation. They take comfort in the idea that their personal assets will be protected from the corporation's creditors. In reality, however, there are several limits on this protection.

2.1a Common-sense limits

People like Sally and Mary who start businesses are practical, careful people. They do not become successful in business by buying more supplies than they can afford or by producing more product than they can sell. Also, suppliers are not stupid. They didn't get to be successful by selling lots of their product or granting huge amounts of credit to new businesses that can't afford to pay them. So in the beginning, at least, limited liability — protection of their personal assets from claims by suppliers and creditors of their business — won't be a big concern to Sally and Mary. If they buy only what they can afford and if they are prompt about paying their bills, limited liability will have little practical significance.

However, as their business grows, limited liability might become very important. As they gain new customers and hire more people, they will inevitably lose direct, personal control over what each and every employee is doing, and over the terms of each and every contract the company makes. Mary and Sally will move from being hands-on operators doing everything themselves to managers of others hired to do things for them. Therefore, limited liability will become more and more relevant.

2.1b A legal limit: The personal guarantee

As I've mentioned, suppliers are not stupid. They know about limited liability. They know that if they deal with small corporations on nothing more than the strength of a promise to pay the bills on time, they might end up with a pile of bad debts and nowhere to turn to collect the money. So, being prudent business people themselves, they look for other assurances of payment.

In the case of small corporations, the most common of these is a personal guarantee from the owners of the corporation — a document that says that if the corporation can't pay, the owners will, and that to back up that promise, the owner's personal assets are available to cover the bill.

For example, let's say that Sally decides to rent a space in a strip mall for the business. She isn't worried about the cost because she knows that limited liability protects her from the company's debts. She assumes the landlord will let the company sign the lease; as a result, she and Mary will not be obligated to cover the rent, even though she has no intention of seeing that happen. After all, she is in business to succeed, not to fail.

She finds a nice spot and calls the landlord to arrange a meeting. They discuss the business, and the landlord finds that he not only likes Sally but he can see that she is a very good, honest person. But that doesn't change the fact that hers is a new company, and the landlord wonders whether or not the company is going to be able to earn enough money every month to pay the rent. To protect himself, the landlord asks Mary and Sally to sign a personal guarantee that obligates them to pay out of their own pockets if the company can't.

Similarly, Mary and Sally may approach their bank for a loan for the company. Banks are not in the business of loaning money unless it can be repaid, and they are on the lookout for small corporations that don't have enough assets to back up their loans. Once again, the bank will ask

Sally and Mary to sign personal guarantees of any loan it gives them.

In this way, when dealing with banks and landlords, the advantage of limited liability is eliminated. Later, when the company has grown to sufficient size that the payment of rent or bank loans is no longer at risk, these personal guarantees are less likely to be needed.

Note that in Alberta, a personal guarantee must be in writing and a certificate of independent legal advice must be attached to it for it to be legal. This means that both Sally and Mary have to go to an independent lawyer to get it signed. They cannot use the bank's lawyer, or the landlord's lawyer, but they can use their own, if they have one.

2.1c   Liability for negligence

Another limit to limited liability that is often misunderstood is liability for acts of personal negligence. Limited liability may protect you from responsibility for business debts that your corporation incurs, but it never protects you from responsibility for negligent acts that cause harm or injury to other people. In other words, if you harm someone, you can't hide behind your company and say that you are not responsible for the damage you caused.

For example, let's say the company buys a car that Mary uses to visit customers. If she runs a red light and hits someone, Mary can't say that it is only the company's responsibility. Mary herself is responsible as the driver of the car, and both Mary and the company will be sued. In reality, the company will have insurance to cover such a loss, but if it didn't, Mary would have to cover it herself, and her personal assets would be available to do that.

The sphere of negligence is a huge area of law. A full discussion of it as it relates to corporations is beyond the scope of this book.

2.1d   An example of limited liability at work

Here is an example of limited liability at work. An employee of Sally and Mary's incorporated company enters into a series of unprofitable contracts or orders unnecessary supplies. If the employee made the deals as part of his or her normal job, the company is responsible and the company will get sued. If the company can't pay the amount owing and is closed down, Sally and Mary will lose only whatever money they put into the company; usually that is the amount they paid for their shares and the amount of any loans they may have made to the company to help it run. But they will not be sued personally, and their personal assets will be protected.

2.2 The advantage of perpetual existence

As we saw, if a sole proprietor or partner dies, the proprietorship or partnership is terminated. Whether or not the business continues will be up to the heirs of the proprietor or the surviving partners.

However, a corporation does not die when one or all of its owners do, nor does a corporation end when an owner decides to get out of the business. That's because corporations have perpetual existence. Like the Energizer Bunny, they just go on, and on, and on. It's business as usual. Any contracts the corporation has with customers and suppliers continue, and so do the debts and other obligations, such as paying the rent or the bank loan.

2.2a   A practical example of perpetual existence

Let's look at what that means for Sally and Mary. What would happen to their corporation if they went on a business trip to Mexico to check out cheaper facilities for making their products, and the plane went down? If they did not survive the crash, their ownership in the company (represented by their shares — I will discuss the specifics of this later) passes under their wills to their heirs. Sally's shares go to her husband, who is a dentist. Mary's shares go to her three children. The company continues, but it now has entirely new owners who may not know anything about the business, who may not have the time or desire to run it, and who may not even get along.

The good news is that they have something to sell: their shares in the successful business that Sally and Mary built up. If they sell their shares, the company carries on. Not only do the new owners benefit from all the hard work Sally and Mary did, they can carry on and continue to make it grow.

The bad news is that there may not be anyone willing to buy the shares. Even though the business is being run through a corporation, it may still be Mary and Sally's business in the eyes of the most important people — the customers. With the two founders gone, the customers might decide to take their business to other people they know, rather than take a chance on new owners they don't know. If that happens, the heirs have no choice but to wind up the company, sell its assets, and pay its debts. If the sale of the corporation's assets doesn't raise enough to cover the debts, at least the heirs are protected from having to pay the excess out of their own pockets, thanks to limited liability. However, they will still have to pay any debts covered by personal guarantees.

Those documents will contain clauses that say they are binding on the heirs and administrators of Sally's and Mary's estates.

You don't have to have a two-person corporation.

I use the example of two people forming a corporation, but under Alberta law there is no limit on the number of people who can incorporate a company. It is even possible for just one person to do so. In fact, every year, a large number of new, one-person corporations come into existence. If you wish to set up a one-person corporation, all you have to do is eliminate the references to the second person in the forms. Simply show yourself as the incorporator, the only director, the owner of all the shares, and the president.

2.3 Tax advantages

Aside from limited liability, possible tax advantages are the most common reason why people want to set up corporations for their business activities. That's because of a tax benefit available to small corporations, called the small-business deduction, that the federal government introduced in 1971 to encourage the development and growth of small businesses. Alberta, which also taxes the income of small corporations, offers a parallel benefit.

The small-business deduction applies to the first $200,000 of active business income that each small, privately owned incorporated business earns each year. Active business income is income earned from the corporation's normal activities, but does not include income from investments. The effect of the combined federal and Alberta deductions is that small-business corporations pay tax at a rate of 19.12 percent on the first $200,000 of active business income.

In its 2000 budget, the federal government introduced a new deduction for the next $100,000 of such income, but Alberta has not yet done the same. The combined rate on income between $200,000 and $300,000 is now 37.62 percent, and income over $300,000 is taxed at a combined rate of 44.62 percent.

2.3a Will you pay less tax?

If your business earns less than $200,000 and your corporation can pay tax at a rate of only 19.12 percent, who wouldn't incorporate? But remember who is paying the tax — your corporation; and remember where the leftover money is — in the corporation. The problem now is how you get it out and into your pocket, and what happens from a tax point of view when you do.

Once again, let's take the example of Mary and Sally. They can take dollars out of their corporation by paying themselves a fair and reasonable salary for the work they do for the corporation, or by taking dividends on their shares, or a combination of both.

If they take a salary, that amount becomes a deduction the corporation can claim, but that amount is income in Sally's and Mary's hands. In fact, the corporation must issue a T4 slip to each of them, and they must declare that amount on their own personal tax return each year. Net result? No savings. If they take dividends, the same result applies. No tax savings. There used to be savings if money was taken out as dividends, but the government has been working hard to tighten up the rules over the past few years in order to eliminate that. So incorporation may not result in a tax saving to Mary and Sally.

2.3b Can you defer tax?

If your corporation is earning more money than you need to live on, and you can afford to leave after-tax income in the company, then you will see a savings, at least until you need to take that money out for yourself. This tax-planning strategy is called tax deferral. The money you leave in the company is taxed at the small-business rate, and the next level of tax (the tax you would pay on it personally if you took it out of the business) is deferred, or delayed, until that money is actually paid out to you as salary or dividends. This strategy is useful if your corporation's income fluctuates from year to year and you want to even out the flow to yourself, and if you can afford to live without any money from the corporation from time to time.

Another deferral strategy available to corporations involves declaring a bonus, which works like this. Let's say Sally and Mary's corporation had a good year in 2000 and earned more than $200,000 in active business income. The company can declare a bonus payable to them in the amount of the excess over $200,000 as long as that amount is reasonable. Then the company can deduct that bonus from its earnings for the year 2000, which brings its active business income down to the 19.12 percent tax level. Of course, that bonus has to be paid to Sally and Mary, and in fact the company can then wait up to 180 days after the end of the year 2000 to pay them. As a result, the bonus is not taxable to them until 2001. By adopting this strategy, Sally and Mary have delayed paying tax on the bonus amount into the next tax year. Whether or not this is a benefit to them depends on their other sources of income for 2001, including any more money they take out of the corporation during that year.

2.3c Can you split tax?

Both of these tax-deferral strategies involve splitting income between two taxable entities — you and your corporation — to get the lowest rate. There are other tax-splitting devices you may be able to use with your corporation, and the most common of these is to split income between family members. If you have a spouse or children who are in lower tax brackets than you are, you can arrange to have your corporation pay dividends to them. Of course, if they are working for the corporation, the corporation can pay them fair and reasonable wages for the work they do.

2.3d Estate-planning opportunities

Corporations can be used to cap the value of a shareholder's interest, which in turn caps the amount that has to be declared for tax purposes when that shareholder dies. The most common strategy for doing this is called an estate freeze, and it works like this.

Let's say Sally and Mary's business flourishes as an unincorporated company, and after only a few years they are offered a half-million dollars for it. They decline to sell, but decide for estate-planning purposes to incorporate their business. They transfer their business to this newly created corporation and take back a special class of shares, called preferred shares, which have a fixed value of $250,000 each.

They also set up the normal kind of shares, called common shares, the value of which will grow as the corporation grows. If Mary and Sally did not also own the common shares, then at their deaths, the value of their interest in the corporation would be frozen at the value of the preferred shares, which is $250,000.

There are many variations on this approach, and Mary and Sally would have to take a number of factors into consideration before doing this, all of which are outside the scope of this discussion. They should consult a lawyer or an accountant, or both.

2.3e Always get professional tax advice

Tax is a complicated technical area, and the information given above is meant to serve only as an introduction. You should always have your own specific situation reviewed by a competent tax adviser before making your decision about the tax advantages of setting up a corporation.

2.4 Complexity

It may be clear by now that setting up a corporation does make life more complex, mainly because that corporation is an independent legal personality that must be maintained and properly cared for. Sally and Mary will soon find that to incorporate, they must set up bank accounts for the company that are separate from their own, keep a separate set of books, and as we shall see, go through the necessary procedures to bring the corporation alive and keep it alive as far as the government is concerned.

They must also see to the preparation and filing of corporate tax returns: one for the federal government, and a separate one for the Alberta Government, because Alberta collects its own corporate income tax.

Sally and Mary must prepare the corporation's annual financial statements, and they must keep track of all the legally required books and records (which I'll discuss in chapter 3).

Above all, they must always remember that they are not the corporation. The corporation is an independent legal entity, and even though they are the instruments that make it function, it is different and distinct from themselves.

2.5 Cost

Sally and Mary must consider the fact that it costs money to start and maintain a corporation. Even if they avoid legal fees by incorporating themselves, they still have to pay the incorporation fees charged by the Alberta government and the fees charged by the private registry offices. They may also need an accountant to help them with bookkeeping and tax returns, and though they may set up the corporation without legal help, they will surely find that they need legal advice as the business develops and the corporation grows.

2.6 Handling Growth

Overriding all these other concerns is the possibility that their business might become very successful. If so, Sally and Mary will need employees, premises, bank loans, and many other business services as well as advisors. They will quickly realize that they are unable to do it all on their own and will need to hire good people to help them, either as employees or as professional advisors. They may also need more people to put money into the business, and that raises the possibility of taking on more shareholders and directors. If the business gets big enough, Sally and Mary may even want to consider selling shares to the general public through a stock exchange. The corporate form of business provides the best way to handle all the challenges brought on by growth.

2.7 Credibility

One of the biggest reasons why people choose to set up a corporation to run their business is credibility. They want to look like serious businesspeople in the eyes of their suppliers and customers, and also in the eyes of lenders, such as the banks. The fact that the business is incorporated makes a positive impression. It says that Sally and Mary are serious about what they are doing, that they have put a significant amount of their own time and money into getting their business started in the most sophisticated way, and that they are confident of success. This will create a good, businesslike impression in the minds of any potential lenders.

3. Five More Things to Know before Incorporating

Mary and Sally have made the decision to incorporate, but there are five more things they need to think about before they start filling out their incorporation papers.

3.1 Federal or provincial incorporation?

Mary and Sally live in Alberta, and their corporation will carry on business in Alberta, so it's obvious they will incorporate in Alberta, right? Of course, but they need to know that there are two incorporation systems available to businesspeople in this province. Both the federal and provincial governments have authority over the incorporation of companies under Canada's constitution, so Sally and Mary can incorporate their Alberta business under the federal system or under the Alberta system. However, they must be aware of the three main differences between these two systems.

3.1a Where the corporation can carry on business

A business incorporated under the federal system is entitled to carry on business in any province or territory in Canada, while a provincially incorporated company can do business only in the province in which it is incorporated. However, this distinction gets watered down in practice, because every federally incorporated company must still file papers and register its existence in each province or territory in which it does business. Similarly, an Alberta corporation that wants to do business in another province or territory can do so by filing the necessary papers with the appropriate authorities.

3.1b Priority over names

Federally incorporated companies do get priority over corporate names. If you want to incorporate under the Alberta system, your proposed corporate name will be rejected if it is the same as or similar to the name of an existing federal corporation.

3.1c Cost

The federal fee for incorporation has always been higher than the fee charged by the Alberta government, and it still is, even though the federal fee was recently reduced from $500 to $300. The Alberta government incorporation fee is $100. You must add to that the fees charged by the private registry outlets in Alberta for processing your papers. Those fees range from $50 to $150.

The fact is that the overwhelming majority of Alberta's small-business people who choose to incorporate use the Alberta system. If they need to, they can always register their Alberta company in one or two neighbouring provinces when the time comes. Mary and Sally are no different, and the rest of this book follows the process for incorporating in Alberta.

3.2 Two types of Alberta corporations

Technically, there are two types of corporations that can be incorporated under the Alberta system, though as you can see from the explanations below, only one of them applies to Mary and Sally.

3.2a Distributing corporations

These are big corporations that have legal authority and permission to sell (or "distribute") their shares to the general public, either directly or through a stock exchange. People buy shares in these companies for two reasons: they hope that the value of the shares will go up as the company prospers and they expect to receive a share of the company's profits in the form of dividends. Sally and Mary aren't playing in this league, so they won't use this kind of corporation.

3.2b   Non-distributing corporations

These are corporations that do not have authority or permission to sell their shares to members of the general public. Non-distributing corporations are divided into two subgroups: those with more than 15 shareholders and those with 15 or fewer shareholders. The main difference between the two is that non-distributing companies with more than 15 shareholders must file a great deal of financial information for the protection of their shareholders.

Since Mary and Sally, like most Alberta businesspeople who incorporate, will be the only shareholders of their corporation, their company falls into the "15 or fewer shareholders" category of a non-distributing corporation, and that is the sort of company with which the remainder of this book will deal.

3.3   Five different roles you must play

This is the point at which the principle of separate legal entity comes to life. Because the corporation will be a distinct legal creature that can act only through the humans who control it, Mary and Sally must have a clear understanding of the different roles they will need to play. These five roles usually apply to everyone who incorporates a business.

3.3a   Shareholder

Shareholders are the owners of the corporation, but they do not own the actual assets of the company. In the case of Sally and Mary, their corporation owns the sewing machines, tables, cloth, supplies, and everything else Mary and Sally will need to carry on business. What Mary and Sally will own are the shares in the company, and those shares give them three important rights:

i)   The right to vote at shareholders' meetings and elect the directors of the corporation

ii) The right to a share of the profits earned by the corporation in the form of dividends

iii) The right to a share of the assets of the corporation if it is wound up

Mary and Sally must pay for these rights, and they do that by buying the shares from the corporation shortly after it is incorporated. While they may choose to pay a large amount for their shares, and by doing so put a lot of money into the corporation's bank account to cover its operating costs, it is more likely that they will pay only a dollar or so for each share. That's because small businesses of this kind do not usually raise the money they need to operate from the sale of shares. Instead, Mary and Sally will probably raise it by borrowing it, either from themselves or from a bank on the strength of a personal guarantee.

As shareholders, Mary and Sally do not have day-to-day control over the operation of their corporation. That power and responsibility is given to the directors. What Mary and Sally do have is the right to elect directors, and to vote them out if they are not doing a good job. Once a year, the directors are required to call an annual general meeting to present information about the corporation's activities to the shareholders, and if they are dissatisfied they can vote for new directors at that time.

The main concern of shareholders is a simple and quite personal one: they just want to know if they are making any money from their shares. The only liability a shareholder might face is the possibility that the corporation might fail and not be able to repay the shareholder the amount he or she paid for the shares. Minimizing that risk is another reason why Mary and Sally will pay only small amounts for their shares. For more information on shareholder agreements and remedies, see chapter 4.

3.3b Director

The directors run the company. In a small corporation, they do everything themselves. In a bigger one, they are free to hire managers to look after different aspects of the corporation's business and report back to them. Sally and Mary will be directors of their corporation and, in the initial stages at least, they will do it all themselves. However, they must realize that directors take on some important responsibilities and liabilities because, unlike shareholders, directors are in a position of trust over the corporation and, to some extent, its employees. They cannot use this position of trust to benefit themselves.

The directors of a corporation, no matter how big or small it may be, must —

i)   act honestly and in good faith, in the best interests of the corporation;

ii) exercise the care and skill of a reasonably prudent person;

iii) disclose any personal interest they may have in any proposed contract with the corporation;

iv) not allow the sale of shares for anything except money; and

v) not issue dividends or sell more shares unless the corporation meets the financial tests set by law.

With respect to employees of the corporation, federal tax law says the directors must make sure the corporation sends in the appropriate amounts that must be withheld for income tax and other federal programs for each employee or face personal liability for any unpaid amounts. (Directors are also liable if the corporation does not send in the necessary amounts for GST.) Also, Alberta law says that directors can be personally liable for up to six months' wages of employees if the corporation is closed down or goes into bankruptcy.

Finally, environmental laws say that directors may be personally responsible for any damage that the corporation causes to the environment as it carries out its business.

Note that under the Alberta incorporation system, directors must be over the age of 18 years, of sound mind, and not in bankruptcy. Also, a director must be a human: a corporation cannot be appointed director of another corporation.

Sally and Mary need not worry about these responsibilities in the early stages of their business, but as it grows, these areas will become much more important, and they should be aware of them.

3.3c Officer

The directors have the right to appoint officers to handle different aspects of the corporation's business. President and secretary-treasurer are two of the most common officers found within corporations.

As far as Sally and Mary are concerned, these titles are largely ceremonial. After all, they will be doing all the work themselves and they will be working closely together on a daily basis. But since Sally thought of the original business idea, she will become president, and Mary will be secretary-treasurer. Also, these titles do give credibility to the operation, and banks in particular like to see them when they make loans to small corporations.

3.3d Employee

In any organization, it's the employees who do the work, and they expect to be paid a fair wage for doing it. Sally and Mary are no different. In the beginning at least, they will be doing everything — taking orders, buying material, sewing product, packing and shipping orders, preparing and sending invoices, collecting payment, depositing and writing cheques — everything that needs to happen to make the business a success. In other words, they will be the employees of the corporation. As directors, they will decide how much they are going to pay themselves, and how often.

3.3e Creditor

As we saw, Mary and Sally will lend money to the corporation so it can cover its operating expenses until it makes enough money to cover them on its own. That makes them creditors of the corporation. This fact becomes important if the corporation can't repay them. They don't get special treatment just because they incorporated the business and because they own the shares. Instead, they are in the same position as anyone else who lends money to the corporation. If the corporation fails, all the creditors share equally in the assets of the corporation, although those who have special protection, such as the personal guarantees we talked about, will be paid first, while the rest of the creditors — including Sally and Mary — will share whatever is left over.

3.4 The importance of shares

Shares are the pieces of paper that represent ownership of a corporation, and they carry with them the three main rights mentioned above: the right to vote, the right to a share of the profits, and the right to a share of the assets on the winding up of the corporation.

Each corporation has the right to issue a certain number of shares, and that number is called the authorized capital of the corporation. That number is found in a document called the articles of incorporation, which I'll discuss in chapter 2. Most corporations do not issue all the authorized shares, and the number of shares actually issued is called the issued share capital.

In theory, the sale of shares is one of the main ways to raise money, or capital, for the corporation's operations, but Mary and Sally are not interested in paying large amounts for their shares. Instead, they will be loaning money to the corporation, and they will also be arranging a line of credit through a bank.

3.4a Two classes of shares

It is important to note that a corporation can issue two different types, or classes, of shares. These are called common shares and preferred shares.

Common shares

These are the basic shares that every corporation must have, and this is the type of share we've been talking about so far in this book. Common shares must always carry all three of the rights mentioned above: the right to vote, the right to a share of the profits, and the right to a share of the assets on winding up. Common shares are usually referred to as Class A shares.

Preferred Shares

A corporation can also issue preferred shares; shares with extra privileges, called preferences, that the common shares don't have. Details of the different types of preferred shares and of the special privileges they contain are also found in the articles of incorporation.

One typical privilege of preferred shares is that they allow the incorporators to split the corporation's income with someone else, usually a spouse, without forcing the incorporators to give up any control over the corporation. The incorporators do that by issuing a class of preferred shares with a preference for payment of a share of the profits, but without any voting rights. Those shares are called Class B shares.

In fact, preferred shares are very flexible and can be designed to suit a number of situations. Each class of preferred shares usually carries one preference, and they are issued in series and called Class B, C, or D shares, as the case may be.

Sally and Mary are not worried about preferred shares right now, but they see that they may need to issue some in the future as the business becomes successful. Therefore, in their articles of incorporation, they are including the right to issue Class B preferred shares.

3.4b Par-value and no-par-value shares

In the past, the value of a corporation's shares, called the par value, could be fixed in the corporation's incorporation documents. Shares that did not have this fixed value were called no-par-value shares. You may still hear these terms, but please note that Alberta law abolished par-value shares quite a few years ago, so Mary and Sally's corporation will have only no-par-value shares. Mary and Sally, as directors of the corporation, will set the value that must be paid to purchase any shares when the shares are issued.

3.5 Pre-incorporation contracts

Since Mary and Sally are already in business, they are presently liable for any contracts they make before the corporation is incorporated. However, they might want to shift liability for any new contracts to the corporation.

For example, they might have a lead on the perfect warehouse and want to nail the space down before someone else does. They should make it clear that they are contracting "on behalf of a corporation to be incorporated," and should write those words on any document they sign. Doing so will give notice to the people or businesses with which they are dealing that once the corporation is in existence, it will have the right to ratify and accept the contract. When it does, Sally and Mary will no longer have any responsibility under that contract. If, for some reason, the corporation doesn't ratify the deal, Sally and Mary remain personally liable. However, as the incorporators, shareholders, and directors, they have the power to make sure it does.

4. Conclusion

There are many reasons why people choose to incorporate their businesses. For Sally and Mary, the decision may come down to nothing more tangible than a conviction that they are going to be successful and a desire to communicate that conviction to the rest of the world. And that is legitimate.

The best advice for anyone considering incorporation is this: if making a living from your business is your main goal, and if you will need all the money from your business to live on, then you don't need a corporation — yet. But if your business will be earning more money than you need, go ahead.

In the long run, a corporation is the proven choice for those who need flexibility, and incorporating will position you to benefit from the growth of your business in ways that sole proprietorship and partnership cannot.

The rest of this book tells you what to do once you are sure that a corporation is right for you.

2
HOW TO INCORPORATE

Now that you have decided that you want to incorporate a company to operate your business, let's look at how to do that, using Mary and Sally as an example. We will examine the process they must follow to select an acceptable name for their corporation and discuss the paperwork required to register their corporation with the appropriate department of the Alberta government. Also, we will examine the role of the private registry offices in this process.

1. Alberta Corporate Registry and the Private Registry System

The Alberta government office that oversees incorporations is called Corporate Registry and it is part of Alberta Government Services. It can be reached through that department's Web site, <www.gov.ab.ca/gs/>.

However, when it comes to incorporating their business, Mary and Sally don't need to worry about finding Corporate Registry's offices, nor about the hours when it is open. During the 1990s, the government of Alberta privatized most registration services, including the registration of incorporation documents, to a network of more than 200 privately owned registries.

The private registry operators are, in fact, agents of the government for the purpose of registering incorporation documents. They have direct access to the government's computers. For example, when they process an incorporation, it automatically goes into the government's data bank. The 2001 Edmonton *Yellow Pages* lists more than six pages of these private registries under "License and Registry Services." Many are open late nights and weekends.

Even though Corporate Registry doesn't provide registration services directly to the public anymore, it does set the procedures, prescribe the forms, and make sure that everything is done in accordance with the law. And it still charges fees for registering documents such as those for an incorporation, but its fees are fixed and are paid by the registry operators each time they register a document.

The private registries make money by charging their own fees over and above the government fee. These private registry fees do vary, so Mary and Sally might want to phone around before deciding which registry office to use. Once they have decided, they simply take their incorporation papers to that private registry and submit them for registration.

2. Choosing a Name for the Corporation

2.1 Using a number for a name

A corporation does not have to have a name. If you wish, you can simply use the incorporation number issued by the Alberta government, followed by the words "Alberta Inc."

For example, if the next number available in the series was 457398, your corporation would be called "457398 Alberta Inc.," and would be referred to as a numbered company. This arrangement is handy when you are in a hurry to get your corporation up and running. Later on, the corporation can change to a name composed of words.

Mary and Sally, however, don't like the idea of their incorporated business being known only as a number, and they don't think that will impress customers, either. They want a name that customers will like and remember, so they will follow the steps described below to obtain and protect a unique name for their corporation.

2.2 Choosing a name

Sally and Mary have been operating quite nicely as "Sally and Mary's Table Trappings," so they want to keep as much of that as possible in their corporate name. But they must keep in mind the fact that a corporation's name has three elements: the distinctive element, the descriptive element, and the legal element. Each of these is described below.

2.2a The distinctive element

This is the original part of the corporate name that distinguishes the corporation from all the others. "Sally's and Mary's Table Trappings" does that, but it's a bit long, while a shorter version, "S & M Table Trappings," suggests something quite inappropriate. Because they know they have to add more words to satisfy the other two elements of a corporate name, they decide to drop their own names altogether and go with "Table Trappings," which is very unusual and distinctive.

2.2b The descriptive element

This element describes the nature of the corporation's business. Mary and Sally choose "Design and Manufacture."

2.2c The legal element

Alberta law requires that every corporate name must end with any one of the following: Limited, Limitée, Ltd., Incorporated, Incorporée, Inc., Corporation, or Corp. Mary and Sally like the sound of "Inc.," so the name they propose for their corporation is "Table Trappings Design & Manufacture Inc."

2.3 Searching and reserving the name

Sally and Mary must now make sure that this name, or a close variation of it, is not already being used in Alberta. To do that, they go to a private registry office and order a NUANS report, which stands for "Newly Updated and Automated Name Search" report.

Private registries charge approximately $50 for a NUANS report, and it is usually available in 24 hours. It covers all corporate and trade names registered in Alberta, those registered to all federally incorporated corporations, and all federally registered trade marks. A copy of the NUANS report for "Table Trappings Design & Manufacture Inc." is included here as Sample 3.

If the proposed name is not in conflict with a name already in use, it is reserved for Mary and Sally for 90 days. If it is in conflict, they will have to come up with a new version of the name that is sufficiently different from the one already in use and try again, or they can approach the owner of the similar name and ask for written permission to incorporate with their version of it.

```
NUANS™REPORT                                              RAPPORT NUANS™

1 "THE PROVISION OF THE INFORMATION CONTAINED IN THIS REPORT IS SUBJECT TO THE
         TERMS AND CONDITIONS CONTAINED ON THE BACK HERE OF."
Industry Canada, NUANS ALBERTA                    WESTEND ETA1143 V=3

? TABLE TRAPPINGS DESIGN & MANUFACTURE INC.   70620245        PAGE 1/6
                                              Alberta         2001 Ma16

================================================================================

TABLE TRAPPINGS DESIGN & MANUFACTURE INC.     AB 70620245      2001Ma16
                                                 PROP. WESTEND

Q-1 DESIGN & MFG. INC.                        CD 3169162         1995Au28
 SASKATOON

TOLE TRAPPINGS                                Ab CRY036153       1979De31
                                                               Partnrship

TABLE MANNERS                                 Ab CRY125848       1986Se10
                                                               Trade_Name

MANUFACTURE DE PAPETERIE BELT LTEE            CD 906875          1974De04
 DOWNSVIEW                                                       1980Au28

TABLE TENNIS GAME FOR THE BLIND LTD.          CD 69697053        2001Ja31
                                                 PROP. FASKEN

MANUFACTURE DE TEXTILE VILENDY INC.           CD 3767647         2000Ma30
 METRO TERRIT

MAMPRINS DRAPERY MANUFACTURING                Ab CRY146169       1987No02
                                                               Trade_Name

MAMPRINS' DRAPERY MANUFACTURING               Ab TN4482253       1989Sell
 CALGARY   T2K 5X2                                             Trade_Name

VILENDY TEXTILE MANUFACTURING INC.            CD 3767647         2000Ma30
 METRO TERRIT

TABLE TENNIS SHOWDOWN LTD.                    CD 69803939        2001Fe12
                                                 PROP. FASKEN

TABLE TENNIS SHOWDOWN LTD.                    CD 69809149        2001Fe13
                                                 PROP. FASKEN

THE DESIGN GROUP INDUSTRIAL STAFFING INC.     Ab 0206525362      1995A127
                                              New_Name Nu1997Oc29 2000No07

BELT STATIONERY MFG LTD.                      CD 906875          1974De04
 DOWNSVIEW                                                       1980Au28

DAYSPRING DESIGN                              Ab CRY045421       1980Oc16
                                                               Trade_Name

DI BIANCHI TILE DESIGN                        Ab TN6199954       1994Au03
 CALGARY   T3C 2B6                                             Trade_Name

VIKTOR SABO LEATHER MANUFACTURING INC.        CD 3763153         2000Ma18
 METRO MONTRE
```

3.   Four Incorporation Documents

Mary and Sally need only four documents to register their new corporation (or only three, if they don't want to give it a name.) These are:

- NUANS report

- Articles of Incorporation

- Notice of Address

- Notice of Directors

3.1   NUANS Report

Mary and Sally must include their NUANS report with the other incorporation documents. Remember, the name is reserved for only 90 days. Fortunately, putting together the other three documents is not a big job. It won't take them long.

3.2   Articles of Incorporation

This form sets out some very basic information about the company. A completed sample is included here as Sample 4. The form is divided into seven parts, with an additional unnumbered section, as follows:

Item 1: Name of corporation

The name Mary and Sally reserved in their NUANS report, "Table Trappings Design & Manufacture Inc.," goes in this field.

Item 2: The classes and maximum number of shares that the corporation is authorized to issue

In this space Mary and Sally set out the different classes of shares they want the company to be able to issue. As mentioned in chapter 1, they want it to have common shares, which carry voting rights, and preferred shares, which do not.

As far as maximum numbers of shares go, there is no reason to limit the number anymore. The government's incorporation fee used to be based on the maximum number of shares a corporation could issue, but that is not true anymore. The government's incorporation fee is the same regardless of the share structure of the corporation.

Mary and Sally will insert the following in Item 2: "An unlimited number of Class A voting shares, and an unlimited number of Class B preferred shares with a preferred cash dividend in an amount to be set by the Directors."

Articles of Incorporation

Business Corporations Act
Section 6

1. Name of Corporation

TABLE TRAPPINGS DESIGN & MANUFACTURING INC.

2. The classes of shares, and any maximum number of shares that the corporation is authorized to issue:

An unlimited number of Class A Voting Shares and an unlimited number of Class B Preferred Shares with a Preferred Cash Dividend in an amount to be set by the directors

3. Restrictions on share transfers (if any):

No shares shall be transferred without the approval of the directors, no shares may be sold to members of the public, and there shall be no more than 15 shareholders at one time

4. Number, or minimum and maximum number, of directors that the corporation may have:

There shall be a minimum of 1 and a maximum of 7 directors

5. If the corporation is restricted FROM carrying on a certain business, or restricted TO carrying on a certain business, specify the restriction(s):

None

6. Other rules or provisions (if any):

None

7. Date authorized by Incorporators: _____ 1 JAN 2001 _____
Year / Month / Day

Incorporators

Name of Person Authorizing *(please print)*	Address: *(including postal code)*
SALLY SMITH	12345 67 AVE. EDMONTON AB A1B 2C3
Identification [DRIVER'S LICENSE #]	
Name of Person Authorizing *(please print)* MARY JONES	Address: *(including postal code)* 12347 67 AVE. EDMONTON AB A1B 2C3
Identification [DRIVER'S LICENSE #]	
Name of Person Authorizing *(please print)*	Address: *(including postal code)*
Identification	
Name of Person Authorizing *(please print)*	Address: *(including postal code)*
Identification	

This information is being collected for the purposes of corporate registry records in accordance with the Business Corporations Act. Questions about the collection of this information can be directed to the Freedom of Information and Protection of Privacy Coordinator for Alberta Registries, Research and Program Support, 3rd Floor, Commerce Place, 10155 - 102 Street, Edmonton, Alberta T5J 4L4, (780) 422-7330.

REG 3047 (99/01)

Item 3: Restrictions on share transfers (*if any*)

As we saw in chapter 1, Sally and Mary want to make sure that their corporation qualifies as a non-distributing corporation with no more than 15 shareholders, so they must state that here by inserting: "No shares shall be transferred without the approval of the Directors, no shares may be sold to members of the public, and there shall be no more than 15 shareholders at one time."

Item 4: Number, or minimum and maximum number, of directors that the corporation may have

At the beginning, there will be only two directors, Sally and Mary, but they want to leave room for the possibility that the corporation may need more directors as it grows. There is no limit on the number of directors it could have, but most new incorporations use this formula: "There shall be a minimum of 1 and a maximum of 7 directors."

Item 5: If the corporation is restricted from carrying on a certain business, or restricted to carrying on a certain business, specify the restrictions.

Years ago, a corporation had to spell out in detail the business it intended to carry on. If it didn't, it ran the risk of not having authority to be involved in different businesses as the opportunities to do so came along. To avoid this situation, incorporators filed a multi-paged list of all possible business activities. Fortunately, the law was changed some years ago, and now a corporation can carry on any business activity unless it is expressly prevented from doing so. For that reason, Mary and Sally need only insert one word here: "None."

Item 6: Other rules or provisions (*if any*)

As far as Mary and Sally are concerned, there are no other rules or provisions that need to be mentioned in this field, so they need only insert the word, "None."

Item 7: Date authorized by Incorporators

The date when the form is completed must be inserted here.

Incorporators

Sally and Mary must insert their own names and addresses. They must also provide proof of their identities, usually a driver's license, in which case the driver's license number is inserted here.

NOTICE OF ADDRESS OR NOTICE OF CHANGE OF ADDRESS

Notice of Address or Notice of Change of Address

Business Corporations Act
Section 19

1. Name of Corporation

2. Corporate Access Number

TABLE TRAPPINGS DESIGN & MANUFACTURING INC.

3. Address of Registered Office *(P.O. Box number **can only** be used by a Society)*

Street	City / Town	Province	Postal Code
9876 54 ST.	EDMONTON	AB	A4D 5E6

OR

Legal Land Description	Section	Township	Range	Meridian

4. Records Address *(P.O. Box number **cannot** be used)*

Street	City / Town	Province	Postal Code
9876 54 ST.	EDMONTON	AB	A4D 5E6

OR

Legal Land Description	Section	Township	Range	Meridian

5. Address for Service by Mail *(If different from Item 3)*

NOTE: *If this is a change, please read instructions carefully.*

Post Office Box Only	City / Town	Province	Postal Code
N/A			

SALLY SMITH	780 123 4567	1 JAN 2001
Name of Person Authorizing *(please print)*	Telephone Number *(daytime)*	Date
[DRIVER'S LICENCE #]		INCORPORATOR
Identification		Title *(please print)*

This information is being collected for the purposes of corporate registry records in accordance with the Business Corporations Act. Questions about the collection of this information can be directed to the Freedom of Information and Protection of Privacy Coordinator for Alberta Registries, Research and Program Support, 3rd Floor, Commerce Place, 10155 - 102 Street, Edmonton, Alberta T5J 4L4, (780) 422-7330.

REG 3016 (99/01)

3.3 Notice of Address or Notice of Change of Address

This form, a sample of which is included here as Sample 5, gives the addresses that must be registered for the corporation. As the name of the form suggests, it has two purposes: it is used by people who are incorporating a new corporation and also by those who wish to change the address for an existing corporation. A brief description of how to complete it follows:

Item 1: Name of Corporation

Insert the name on the NUANS report.

Item 2: Corporate Access Number

Leave this blank. Corporate Registry will fill it in. It is the code number that they use to identify the company.

Item 3: Address of Registered Office

This is the legal address for the company. It is the address to which any legal documents relating to the company will be delivered, and where most mail will be sent. In the case of Mary and Sally, they will use the address of the warehouse they are renting, because that is where they will have their offices and where their staff will be during working hours.

Item 4: Record Address

This is the place where the corporation's important documents, such as these incorporation documents, will be kept. It must be an office that is open to the public during business hours. Mary and Sally will use the warehouse office for the above reasons.

Item 5: Address for Service by Mail (*if different from Item 3*)

This is useful if Mary and Sally wish to give a special address for "service," or delivery, of important legal documents that require a quick and professional response, such as those documents that represent the beginning of a law suit against the corporation. Many incorporators want those documents to go straight to their lawyer's office, so that is the address they enter here. Mary and Sally have decided they don't need a lawyer right now, so they will just put "N/A" in this space.

Bottom of form: Name, telephone number, date, identification, title

Either Mary or Sally can complete this portion as required. For "title," they can say "incorporator," which is what they are until the corporation is officially registered and they hold the meetings necessary to give themselves the other titles they will be assuming.

3.4 Notice of Directors or Notice of Change of Directors

This is another form that is used to incorporate a new corporation. It is also used by existing corporations to give notice to Corporate Registry of a change of directors. A sample is included here as Sample 6, and a brief description of how to complete the form follows.

Item 1: Name of corporation

Insert the NUANS name.

Item 2: Alberta Corporate Access Number

Leave blank. Corporate Registry will insert the next available number in their series.

Item 3: The following persons were appointed Director(s) on

_____

Leave blank. This space is used when an existing corporation wants to add new directors.

Item 4: The following persons ceased to hold office as Director(s) on

_____

Leave blank. This is used when a director of an existing corporation resigns.

Item 5: As of this date, the Directors of the corporation are

Since the corporation doesn't officially exist yet, no one has authority to act on its behalf and no shareholders exist to properly elect the directors. The law gets around this problem by making the incorporators the first directors of the corporation, and that's why Mary and Sally can put their names and addresses in this space on this form.

Also, the law says that at least half of the directors of any Alberta corporation must live in Canada, so Mary and Sally must indicate their residency status here.

As we will see in the next chapter, the authority of the first directors continues through the incorporation process until the shareholders hold their first meeting and formally elect the directors of the corporation.

Item 6: To be completed only by Alberta Corporations

Since Mary and Sally are both resident Canadians, they will mark "Yes" next to the question regarding residency of the directors.

SAMPLE 6
NOTICE OF DIRECTORS OR NOTICE OF CHANGE OF DIRECTORS

Notice of Directors or
Notice of Change of Directors

Business Corporations Act
Sections 101, 108 and 276

1. Name of Corporation

TABLE TRAPPINGS DESIGN & MANUFACTURING INC.

2. Alberta Corporate Access Number

3. The following persons were appointed Director(s) on _____ year / month / day _____ :

Name of Director (Last, First, Second)	Mailing Address (including postal code)	Are you a resident Canadian? Yes	No
		☐	☐
		☐	☐
		☐	☐

4. The following persons ceased to hold office as Director(s) on _____ year / month / day _____ :

Name of Director (Last, First, Second)	Mailing Address (including postal code)

5. As of this date, the Director(s) of the corporation are:

Name of Director (Last, First, Second)	Mailing Address (including postal code)	Are you a resident Canadian? Yes	No
SMITH, SALLY	12345 67 AVE. EDMONTON AB A1B 2C3	✔	☐
JONES, MARY	12347 67 AVE. EDMONTON AB A1B 2C3	✔	☐
		☐	☐
		☐	☐

6. To be completed only by Alberta Corporations:
Are at least half of the members of the Board of Directors resident Canadians? ✔ Yes ☐ No

SALLY SMITH	780 123 4567	1 JAN 2001
Name of Person Authorizing (please print)	Telephone Number (daytime)	Date

[DRIVER'S LICENSE #]	INCORPORATOR
Identification	Title (please print)

This information is being collected for the purposes of corporate registry records in accordance with the Business Corporations Act. Questions about the collection of this information can be directed to the Freedom of Information and Protection of Privacy Coordinator for Alberta Registries, Research and Program Support, 3rd Floor, Commerce Place, 10155 - 102 Street, Edmonton, Alberta T5J 4L4, (780) 422-7330.

REG 3017 (99/01)

Bottom of form: Name, telephone number, date, identification, title

Sally or Mary will include the same information here as on the previous form.

4. Congratulations! It's a Corporation!

It takes about three or four days for the private registry operators to process these four documents and for Corporate Registry to confirm the existence of Mary and Sally's baby, a brand new Alberta corporation called "Table Trappings Design and Manufacture Inc." Proof that the corporation is alive and well comes in the form of a Certificate of Incorporation, which the registry operator gives to Mary and Sally, along with filed copies of the Notice of Address, Notice of Directors, and Articles of Incorporation. A sample of a Certificate of Incorporation for Mary and Sally's corporation is included here as Sample 7.

Sally and Mary are ecstatic, of course, but their work isn't done yet. While this is the end of their involvement with the registry system, it isn't the end of their work as incorporators. The next chapter talks about what they have to do to get their corporation ready for business.

12345678
Corporate Access No.

BUSINESS CORPORATION ACT

Form 2

CERTIFICATE OF INCORPORATION

TABLE TRAPPINGS DESIGN & MANUFACTURE INC.
Name of Corporation

I HEREBY CERTIFY THAT THE ABOVE-MENTIONED CORPORATION, THE ARTICLES

OF INCORPORATION OF WHICH ARE ATTACHED, WAS INCORPORATED UNDER THE

BUSINESS CORPORATIONS ACT OF THE PROVINCE OF ALBERTA.

Signature
Registrar of Corporations

JANUARY 5, 2001
Date of Incorporation

3
AFTER YOU INCORPORATE

As you can see, the procedure for incorporating a company is fairly easily completed. But there are a number of things that must be done to get a corporation ready to do business, and to keep it up and running.

1.   Organizational Meetings and Minute Books

The corporation may now exist in the eyes of the law, but it is no more than an empty shell at this point because it has no internal organization. A lot needs to be done before it is ready for business, and that is what Mary and Sally must turn their attention to now. The first step they must take is to meet in their temporary capacity as first directors to take care of some important organizational business.

1.1 Organizational meeting of first directors

As soon as possible after the incorporation of a company, the first directors must meet to deal with a number of important items of corporate business. The most important ones are adopting the rules that will govern the internal operation of the corporation, appointing the corporate officers, and getting the shares issued to themselves as shareholders, but there are a few other corporate housekeeping items they must take care of.

At this meeting, the first directors must make the necessary resolutions, vote on them, pass them, and keep written minutes of what they are doing. Fortunately, Mary and Sally do not have to do this on their own. They can use a standard set of minutes, included here as Sample 8.

The first few paragraphs of these minutes are self-explanatory, but some sections need comment:

1.1a   Adopt Bylaw 1

Mary and Sally have to adopt a constitution for the corporation; a set of rules that govern almost any situation that might arise as the corporation and its shareholders, directors, and officers go about its business. This constitution is called a by-law; and a standard corporate by-law, called By-law No. 1, has been developed by lawyers to handle almost every conceivable situation that might arise. A copy of By-law No. 1 is included here as Sample 9.

You will understand the importance of this by-law by reviewing its headings. It is not necessary for me to comment on every part of it, but there are three features that do deserve some explanation; the first because it affects the balance of power in terms of voting, and the other two because they give the shareholders and directors freedom from face-to-face meetings:

- *Casting vote to chair:* The directors and the shareholders of an incorporated company have the right to vote on matters of importance to the running of the business. In the event that Mary and Sally do not agree on an issue, the by-law provides a way to break the tie: it gives the chair an extra vote, called a "casting vote." Provision for this is found in section 5.08 for directors' meetings and in section 8.16 for shareholders' meetings.

- *Telephone meetings:* Directors may meet by phone instead of in person, thanks to section 5.09. Section 8.11 grants the same right to shareholders.

- *Written resolutions in lieu of meetings:* Decisions can be made without calling a meeting if a written resolution or minute confirming the decision is signed by all the directors (section 5.10) or shareholders (section 8.20) who have the right to attend and vote.

1.1b   Adopt Share Certificate

This item simply refers to the adoption of the form that the corporation will use for the share certificates it will issue. See Sample 10 for an example of a share certificate.

Minutes of Organizational Meeting of First Directors

Minutes of a Meeting of the First Directors of TABLE TRAPPINGS DESIGN & MANUFACTURE INC.

(Referred to as "the corporation") held at EDMONTON, Alberta, on the 10th day of JANUARY 20 01

SALLY SMITH AND MARY JONES, the incorporators and first directors of the corporation, were present. The chair advised that the corporation was officially incorporated on the

5TH of JANUARY 20 01, and the directors passed the following resolutions:

1) By-law Number 1, a copy of which is attached as Item A, was adopted.

2) The form of share certificate marked as Item B was adopted.

3) The corporate seal, a sample of which was impressed in the margin of these minutes, was adopted.

4) The following were appointed as officers of the corporation with full authority to sign documents for the corporation and to affix the corporate seal as required:

    SALLY SMITH, President

    MARY JONES, Secretary Treasurer

5) The following shares were issued:

    SALLY SMITH, 100 class A shares at $1.00 per share

    MARY JONES, 100 class A shares at $1.00 per share

    Payment was received and the following share certificates were issued:

    Certificate #1 to SALLY SMITH

    Certificate #2 to MARY JONES

6) The CANADIAN Bank was appointed banker for the corporation and the officers were authorized to sign any documents or resolutions required by the bank.

7) The corporation will not appoint an auditor. BILL ROY was appointed accountant for the corporation.

8) The Certificate of Incorporation and other incorporation documents above shall be filed in the corporate minute book.

9) By signing this minute, the first directors waive notice of this meeting and ratify all business transacted.

There being no further business, the meeting was adjourned.

Sally Smith
President

Mary Jones
Secretary Treasurer

ITEM A

BY-LAW NO. 1

A by-law relating generally to the conduct of the affairs of

TABLE TRAPPINGS DESIGN & MANUFACTURE INC.

BE IT ENACTED AND IT IS HEREBY ENACTED as a by-law of

the said Corporation

(hereinafter called the "Corporation") as follows:

Division One
INTERPRETATION

1.01   In this by-law and all other by-laws of the Corporation, unless the context otherwise specifies or requires:

"Act" means the Business Corporations Act of Alberta, as from time to time amended and every statute that may be substituted therefor and, in the case of such substitution, any references in the by-laws of the Corporation to provisions of the Act shall be read as references to the substituted provisions thereof in the new statute or statutes;

"Appoint" includes "elect" and vice versa;

"Articles" means the Articles of Incorporation of the Corporation filed 1 JANUARY 2001 as from time to time amended, supplemented or restated;

"Board" means the board of directors of the Corporation;

"By-laws" means this by-law and all other by-laws of the Corporation from time to time in force and effect;

"Cheque" includes a draft;

"Meeting of Shareholders" includes an annual or other general meeting of shareholders and a special meeting of shareholders; "special meeting of shareholders" includes a meeting of any class or classes of shareholders;

"Recorded Address" means in the case of a shareholder his address as recorded in the securities register; and in the case of joint shareholders the address appearing in the securities register in respect of such joint holding or the first address so appearing if there is more than one; and in the case of a director, officer, auditor or member of a committee of the board, his latest address as recorded in the records of the Corporation;

"Regulations" means the regulations under the Act as published or from time to time amended and every regulation that may be substituted therefor and, in the case of such substitution, any references in the by-laws of the Corporation to provisions of the Regulations shall be read as references to the substituted provisions therefor in the new regulations;

"Resident Albertan" means an individual who is ordinarily resident in Alberta or, if not ordinarily resident in Alberta, is a member of a class of persons prescribed by Regulations and, in any case,

(a)   is a Canadian citizen, or

(b)   has been lawfully admitted to Canada for permanent residence;

"Signing Officer" means, in relation to any instrument, any person authorized to sign the same on behalf of the corporation by virtue of Section 3.01 of this by-law or by a resolution passed pursuant thereto;

SELF-COUNSEL PRESS–CDN-INC-ALT (4-1)01

"Unanimous Shareholder Agreement" means an otherwise lawful written agreement among all shareholders of the corporation, or among all such shareholders and a person who is not a shareholder, that restricts, in whole or in part, the powers of the directors to manage the business and affairs of the Corporation as from time to time amended.

Save as aforesaid, all terms which are contained in the by-laws of the Corporation and which are defined in the Act or the Regulations shall have the meanings given to such terms in the Act or the Regulations. Words importing the singular number include the plural and vice versa; the masculine shall include the feminine; and the word "person" shall include an individual, partnership, association, body corporate, corporation, company, syndicate, trustee, executor, administrator, legal representative, and any number or aggregate of persons.

Division Two

BORROWING, BANKING AND SECURITIES

2.01 Borrowing Power: Without limiting the borrowing powers of the Corporation as set forth in the Act, but subject to the articles and any unanimous shareholder agreement, the board may from time to time on behalf of the Corporation, without authorization of the shareholders:

(a) borrow money upon the credit of the Corporation;

(b) issue, reissue, sell or pledge bonds, debentures, note or other evidences of indebtedness or guarantee of the Corporation, whether secured or unsecured;

(c) to the extent permitted by the Act, give a guarantee on behalf of the Corporation to secure performance of any present or future indebtedness, liability or obligation of any person; and

(d) mortgage, hypothecate, pledge or otherwise create a security interest in all or any currently owned or subsequently acquired real or personal, moveable or immoveable, property of the Corporation including book debts, rights, powers, franchises and undertakings, to secure any such bonds, debentures, note or other evidences of indebtedness or guarantee or any other present or future indebtedness, liability or obligation of the Corporation.

Nothing in this section limits or restricts the borrowing of money by the Corporation on bills of exchange or promissory notes made, drawn, accepted or endorsed by or on behalf of the Corporation.

2.01A (a) Raise and assist in raising money for, and to add by way of bonus, loan, promise, endorsement, guarantee or otherwise any person or Company whether or not the Company has business relations with that person or Company and to guarantee the performance or fulfillment of any contracts or obligations of any such person or Company, and in particular to guarantee the payment of the principal of and interest on securities, mortgages and liabilities of any such person or Company;

(b) The Directors may delegate the powers contained in this Article such Officers or Directors of the Corporation and to such extent and in such manner as may be set out in the by-laws;

(c) Lend to or guarantee, with or without security, the contracts of any person or Company, wheresoever incorporated, having dealings or business relations with the Corporation or with whom the Corporation proposes to have dealings or business relations, the contracts of any person or company proposing to buy or owning shares of the capital stock of the Corporation securing or evidencing an obligation in respect of the purchase price thereof or facilitating or evidencing any borrowing by such person or Company in respect of the purchase price of such shares, or otherwise.

2.02 Delegation: The board may from time to time delegate to a committee of the board, a director or an officer of the Corporation or any other person as may be designated by the board all or any of the powers conferred on the board by the preceding section of this by-law or by the Act to such extent and in such manner as the board may determine at the time of such delegation.

2.03 Banking Arrangements: The banking business of the Corporation including, without limitation, the borrowing of money and the giving of security therefore, shall be transacted with such banks, trust companies or other bodies corporate or organizations as may from time to time be designated by or under the authority of the board. Such banking business or any part thereof shall be transacted under such agreements, instructions and delegations of powers as the board may from time to time prescribe.

2.04 Custody of Securities: All shares and securities owned by the Corporation shall be lodged (in the name of the Corporation) with a chartered bank or a trust company or in a safety deposit box or, if so authorized by resolution of the board of directors, with such other depositaries or in such other manner as may be determined from time to time by the board of directors.

SELF-COUNSEL PRESS—CDN-INC-ALT (4-2)01

All share certificates, bonds, debentures, notes or other obligations belonging to the Corporation may be held in the name of a nominee or nominees of the Corporation (and if held in the names of more than one nominee shall be held in the names of the nominees jointly with the right of survivorship) and shall be endorsed in blank with endorsement guaranteed in order to enable transfer to be completed and registration to be effected.

2.05 Voting Shares and Securities in Other Corporations: All of the shares or other securities carrying voting rights of any other body corporate held from time to time by the Corporation, other than shares it beneficially owns in its holding body corporate, may be voted at any and all meetings of shareholders, bondholders, debenture holder or holders of other securities (as the case may be) of such body corporate and in such manner and by such person or persons as the board of directors of the Corporation shall from time to time determine. The proper signing officers of the Corporation may also execute and deliver for and on behalf of the Corporation proxies and/or arrange for the issuance of voting certificates and/ or other evidence of the right to vote in such names as they may determine without the necessity of a resolution or other action by the board of directors.

Division Three
EXECUTION OF INSTRUMENTS

3.01 Deeds, transfers, assignments, contracts, obligations, certificates and other instruments may be signed on behalf of the Corporation by two persons, one of whom holds the office of chairman of the board, managing director, president, vice-president or director and the other of whom holds one of the said offices or the office of secretary, treasurer, assistant secretary or assistant treasurer or any other office created by by-law or by the board. In addition, the board or the said two persons may from time to time direct the manner in which and the person or persons by whom any particular instrument or class of instruments may or shall be signed. Any signing officer may affix the corporate seal to any instrument requiring the same, but no instrument is invalid merely because the corporate seal is not affixed thereto.

3.02 Cheques, Drafts and Notes: All cheques, drafts or orders for the payment of money and all notes and acceptances and bills of exchange shall be signed by such officer or officers or person or persons, whether or not officers of the Corporation, and in such manner as the board of directors may from time to time designate by resolution.

Division Four
DIRECTORS

4.01 Number: The board of directors shall consist of the number fixed by the articles, or where the articles specify a variable number, the number of directors shall be a minimum of one (1) and a maximum of_____7_____, at least half of whom shall be resident Canadians.

4.02 Election and Term: Subject to the articles or a unanimous shareholder agreement the election of directors shall take place at each annual meeting of shareholders and all the directors then in office, unless elected for a longer period of time, shall retire but, if qualified, shall be eligible for re-election. The number of directors to be elected at any such meeting shall, subject to the articles or a unanimous shareholder agreement, be the number of directors then in office, or the number of directors whose terms of office expire at the meeting, as the case may be, except that if cumulative voting is not required by the articles and the articles otherwise permit, the shareholders may resolve to elect some other number of directors. Where the shareholders adopt an amendment to the articles to increase the number or minimum number of directors, the shareholders may, at the meeting at which they adopt the amendment, elect the additional number of directors authorized by the amendment. If an election of directors is not held at the proper time, the incumbent directors shall continue in office until their successors are elected. If the articles provide for cumulative voting each director elected by shareholders (but not directors elected or appointed by creditors or employees) ceases to hold office at the annual meeting and every shareholder entitled to vote at an election of directors has the right to cast votes for the directors to be elected equal to the number of votes attached to the shares held by him multiplied by the number of directors he is entitled to vote for, and he may cast all such votes in favor of one candidate or distribute them among the candidates in such manner as he sees fit. If he has voted for more than one candidate without specifying the distribution among such candidates he shall be deemed to have divided his votes equally among the candidates for whom he voted.

4.03 Removal of Directors: Subject to the Act, the shareholders may by ordinary resolution passed at a meeting specially called for such purpose remove any director from office, except a director elected by employees or creditors pursuant to the articles or a unanimous shareholder agreement, and the vacancy created by such removal may be filled at the same meeting, failing which it may be filled by the board. Provided, however, that if the articles provide for cumulative voting no director shall be removed pursuant to this section where the votes cast against the resolution for his removal would, if cumulatively voted at an election of the full board, be sufficient to elect one or more directors.

SELF-COUNSEL PRESS–CDN-INC-ALT (4-3)01

4.04 Qualification: No person shall be qualified for election as a director if he is less than 18 years of age; if he is of unsound mind and has been so found by a Court in Canada or elsewhere, if he is not an individual; or if he has the status of a bankrupt. A director need not be a shareholder.

4.05 Consent: No election or appointment of a person as director shall be effective unless:

(a) he was present at the meeting when he was elected or appointed and did not refuse to act as a director, or

(b) he consents in writing to act as a director before his election or appointment or within ten days thereafter, or

(c) he acts as a director pursuant to the election or appointment.

4.06 Vacation of Office: A director ceases to hold office when he dies; he is removed from office by the shareholders or by creditors or employees who elected him, as the case may be; he ceases to be qualified for election as a director; he be convicted of an indictable offence; or his written resignation is sent or delivered to the Corporation, or, if a time is specified in such resignation, at the time so specified, whichever is later.

4.07 Committee of Directors: The directors may appoint from among their number one or more committees of directors, however designated, and subject to Section 110 of the Act may delegate to any such committee any of the powers of the directors. At least half of the members of any such committee shall be resident Canadians.

4.08 Transaction of Business: Subject to the provisions of Section 5.09 the powers of a committee of directors may be exercised by a meeting at which a quorum is present or by resolution in writing signed by all the members of such committee who would have been entitled to vote on that resolution at a meeting of the committee. Meetings of such committee may be held at any place in or outside Canada.

4.09 Advisory Bodies: The board may from time to time appoint such advisory bodies as it may deem advisable, but the functions of any such other committees shall be advisory only.

4.10 Procedure: Unless otherwise determined by the board, each committee and advisory body shall have the power to fix its quorum at not less than a majority of its members, to elect its chairman and to regulate its procedure.

4.11 Remuneration and Expenses: Subject to any unanimous shareholder agreement, the directors shall be paid such remuneration for their services as the board may from time to time determine. The directors shall also be entitled to be reimbursed for travelling and other expenses properly incurred by them in attending meetings of the board or any committee thereof. Nothing herein contained shall preclude any director from serving the Corporation in any other capacity and receiving remuneration therefor.

4.12 Subscribers first directors: The subscribers hereto shall be the first directors of the Corporation, unless the Corporation has been incorporated and directors elected prior to the adoption of these articles.

4.13 Alternate directors: Any director may, at any time and from time to time, appoint any other person to be his alternate to act in his place at any meeting of directors at which he is not personally present, and may at any time remove any alternate director appointed by him and appoint another in his place. The notice of appointment may name more than one person in order of preference to act as alternate, if the other persons named in priority are not present at any meeting. An alternate director shall not be entitled to receive any notice of meetings of directors or any remuneration from the Corporation, but he shall otherwise have the powers and be subject in all respects to the terms and conditions existing with reference to the other directors of the Corporation. Any appointment so made may be revoked at any time by the appointor. An alternate director shall, ipso facto, cease to be an alternate director if his appointor ceases for any reason to be a director. Every person acting as an alternate director shall alone be responsible to the Corporation for his own acts and defaults, and he shall not be deemed to be the agent of or for the director appointing him. The director so appointing shall not be responsible for the acts and defaults of an alternate director so appointed. All appointments and removals of alternate directors made by any director in pursuance of this by-law shall be in writing under the name of the director making the same, and shall be sent to or left at the registered office or the head office of the Corporation or sent to or delivered to the Secretary of the Corporation. Any appointment of an alternate director may be either for a specific meeting or for all meetings during a specific period of time.

Division Five

MEETING OF DIRECTORS

5.01   Place of Meeting: Meetings of the board of directors and of committees of directors (if any) may be held within or outside Alberta.

5.02   Notice of Meeting: Notice of the time and place of each meeting of the board shall be given in the manner provided in Section 13.01 to each director not less than 48 hours before the time when the meeting is to be held. A notice of a meeting of directors need not specify the purpose of or the business to be transacted at the meeting except where the Act requires such purpose or business to be specified, including, if required by the Act, any proposal to:

(a)   submit to the shareholders any question or matter requiring approval of the shareholders;

(b)   fill a vacancy among the directors or in the office of auditor;

(c)   issue securities;

(d)   declare dividends;

(e)   purchase, redeem or otherwise acquire shares issued by the Corporation;

(f)   pay a commission for the sale of shares;

(g)   approve a management proxy circular;

(h)   approve a take-over bid circular or directors' circular;

(i)   approve any annual financial statements; or

(j)   adopt, amend or repeal by-laws.

Provided, however, that a director may in any manner waive notice of a meeting and attendance of a director at a meeting of directors shall constitute a waiver of notice of the meeting except where a director attends a meeting for the express purpose of objecting to the transaction of any business on the grounds that the meeting is now lawfully called.

For the first meeting of the board of directors to be held immediately following an election of directors or for a meeting of the board of directors at which a director is to be appointed to fill a vacancy in the board, no notice of such meeting shall be necessary to the newly elected or appointed director or directors in order to legally constitute the meeting, provided that a quorum of the directors is present.

5.03   Adjourned Meeting: Notice of an adjourned meeting of the board is not required if the time and place of the adjourned meeting is announced at the original meeting.

5.04   Regular Meetings: The board may appoint a day or days in any month or months for regular meetings of the board at a place and hour to be named. A copy of any resolution of the board fixing the place and time of such regular meetings shall be sent to each director forthwith after being passed, and forthwith to each director subsequently elected or appointed, but no other notice shall be required for any such regular meeting except where the Act or this by-law requires the purpose thereof or the business to be transacted thereat to be specified.

5.05   Chairman and Secretary: The Chairman of any meeting of the board shall be the first mentioned of such of the following officers as have been appointed and who is a director and is present at the meeting: chairman of the board, managing director or president. If no such officer is present, the directors present shall choose one of their number to be chairman. The secretary of the Corporation shall act as secretary at any meeting of the board, and if the secretary of the Corporation be absent, the chairman of the meeting shall appoint a person who need not be a director to act as secretary of the meeting.

5.06   Quorum: Subject to the following section, the quorum for the transaction of business at any meeting of the board shall consist of a majority of the directors holding office or such greater number of directors as the board may from time to time determine.

5.07   Half Canadian Representation at Meetings: The Board shall not transact business at a meeting, other than filling a vacancy in the Board, unless at least half of the directors present are resident Canadians, except where:

(a)   a resident Canadian director who is unable to be present approves in writing or by telephone or other telecommunication facilities the business transacted at the meeting; and

(b)   at least half of the members present would have been resident Canadians had that director been present at the meeting.

5.08   Voting: Questions arising at any meeting of the board of directors shall be decided by a majority of votes. In case of an equality of votes the chairman of the meeting, in addition to his original vote, shall have a second or casting vote.

5.09   Meeting by Telephone: If all the directors of the Corporation consent, a director may participate in a meeting of the board or a committee of the board by means of such telephone or other communication facilities as permit all persons participating in the meeting to hear each other, and a director participating in such a meeting by such means is deemed to be present at the meeting. Any such consent shall be effective whether given before or after the meeting to which it relates and may be given with respect to all meetings of the board and of committees of the board.

5.10   Resolution in Lieu of Meeting: Notwithstanding any of the foregoing provisions of this by-law, a resolution in writing either ordinary or special, signed by all the Directors entitled to vote on that resolution at a meeting of the directors or a committee of directors, if any is as valid as if it had been passed at a meeting of the directors or the committee of directors, if any.

5.11   Minutes: Minutes of any meeting of the board or of any committee of the board, if purporting to be signed by the chairman of such meeting or by the chairman of the next succeeding meeting, shall be receivable as prima facie evidence of the matters stated in such minutes.

5.12   Management and business vested in the board: The management and conduct of the business and affairs of the Corporation shall be vested in the board, which, in addition to the powers and authorities by these by-laws or otherwise expressly conferred upon it, may exercise all such powers and do all such acts and things as may be exercised or done by the Corporation and are not hereby or by statute expressly directed or required to be exercised or done by the members.

Division Six

PROTECTION OF DIRECTORS, OFFICERS AND OTHERS

6.01   Conflict of Interest: A director or officer shall not be disqualified by his office, or be required to vacate his office, by reason only that he is a party to, or is a director or officer or has a material interest in any person who is a party to, a material contract or proposed material contract with the Corporation or a subsidiary thereof. Such a director or officer shall, however, disclose the nature and extent of his interest in the contract at the time and in the manner provided by the Act. Any such contract or proposed contract shall be referred to the board or shareholders for approval even if such contract is one that in the ordinary course of the Corporation's business would not require approval by the board or shareholders. Subject to the provisions of the Act, a director shall not by reason only of his office be accountable to the Corporation or to its shareholders for any profit or gain realized from such a contract or transaction, and such contract or transaction shall not be void or voidable by reason only of the director's interest therein, provided that the required declaration and disclosure of interest is properly made, the contract or transaction is approved by the directors or shareholders, and it is fair and reasonable to the Corporation at the time it was approved and, if required by the Act, the director refrains from voting as a director on the contract or transaction and absents himself from the director's meeting at which the contract is authorized or approved by the directors, except attendance for the purpose of being counted in the quorum.

6.02   Limitation of Liability: Every director and officer of the Corporation in exercising his powers and discharging his duties shall act honestly and with good faith with a view to the best interests of the Corporation and exercise the care, diligence and skill that a reasonably prudent person would exercise in comparable circumstances. Subject to the foregoing, no director or officer for the time being of the Corporation shall be liable for the acts, receipts, neglects or defaults of any other director or officer or employee or for joining in any receipt or act for conformity, or for any loss, damage or expense happening to the Corporation through the insufficiency or deficiency of title to any property acquired by the Corporation or for or on behalf of the Corporation for the insufficiency or deficiency of any security in or upon which any of the moneys of or belonging to the Corporation shall be placed out or invested or for any loss, conversion, misapplication or misappropriation of or any damage resulting from any dealings with any moneys, securities or other assets belonging to the Corporation or for any other loss, damage or misfortune whatever which may happen in the execution of the duties of his respective office or trust or in relation thereto; provided that nothing herein shall relieve any director or officer from the duty to act in accordance with the Act and the regulations thereunder or from liability for any breach thereof. The directors for the time being of the Corporation shall not be under any duty or responsibility in respect of any contract, act or transaction whether or not made, done or entered into the name or on behalf of the Corporation, except such as shall have been submitted to and authorized or approved by the board of directors.

6.03 **Indemnity:** Subject to the Section 119 of the Act, the Corporation shall indemnify a director or officer, a former director or officer, or a person who acts or acted at the Corporation's request as a director or officer of a body corporate of which the Corporation is or was a shareholder or creditor, and his heirs, executors, administrators and other legal representatives, from and against,

    (a)   any liability and all costs, charges and expenses that he sustains or incurs in respect of any action, suit or proceeding that is proposed or commenced against him for or in respect of anything done or permitted by him in respect of the execution of the duties of his office; and

    (b)   all other costs, charges and expenses that he sustains or incurs in respect of the affairs of the Corporation;

except where such liability relates to his failure to act honestly and in good faith with a view to the best interests of the Corporation.

The Corporation shall also indemnify such persons in such other circumstances as the Act permits or requires. Nothing in this section shall limit the right of any person entitled to indemnity to claim indemnity apart from the provisions of this section.

6.04 **Insurance:** Subject to the Act, the Corporation may purchase and maintain insurance for the benefit of any person referred to in the preceding section against any liability incurred by him in his capacity as a director or officer of the Corporation or of any body corporate where he acts or acted in that capacity at the Corporation's request.

6.05 **Submission of Contracts or Transactions to Shareholders for Approval:** The board of directors in its discretion may submit any contract, act or transaction for approval or ratification at any annual meeting of the shareholders or at any special meeting of the shareholders called for the purpose of considering the same and, subject to the provisions of Section 115 of the Act, any such contract, act or transaction that shall be approved or ratified or confirmed by a resolution passed by a majority of the votes cast at any such meeting (unless any different or additional requirement is imposed by the Act or by the Corporation's articles or any other by-law) shall be as valid and as binding upon the Corporation and upon all the shareholders as though it had been approved, ratified or confirmed by every shareholder of the Corporation.

6.06 **Action by the Board:** Subject to any unanimous shareholder agreement, the board shall manage the business and affairs of the Corporation. The powers of the board may be exercised at a meeting (subject to Sections 4.08 and 4.09) at which a quorum is present or by resolution in writing signed by all the directors entitled to vote on that resolution at a meeting of the board. Where there is a vacancy in the board, the remaining directors may exercise all the powers of the board so long as a quorum remains in office. Where the Corporation has only one director, that director may constitute a meeting.

6.07 **Vacancies:** Subject to the Act, a quorum of the board may fill a vacancy in the board, except a vacancy resulting from an increase in the number or minimum number of directors or from a failure of the shareholders to elect the number or minimum number of directors. In the absence of a quorum of the board, or if the vacancy has arisen from a failure of the shareholders to elect the number or minimum number of directors, the board shall forthwith call a special meeting of the shareholders to fill the vacancy. If the board fails to call such meeting or if there are no such directors then in office, any shareholder may call the meeting.

6.08 **Calling of Meetings:** Meetings of the board shall be held from time to time and at such place as the board, the chairman of the board, the managing director, the president or any two directors may determine.

Division Seven

OFFICERS

7.01 **Election or Appointment:** Subject to any unanimous shareholder agreement, the board from time to time shall elect or appoint a president or a secretary or both, and may elect or appoint one or more vice-presidents (to which title may be added words indicating seniority or function), a general manager, a treasurer and such other officers as the board may determine, including one or more assistants to any of the officers so elected or appointed. The board from time to time may also elect or appoint a chairman of the board, who must be a director and a resident Albertan, but otherwise the officers of the Corporation need not be resident Albertans or directors of the Corporation. Two or more offices may be held by the same person. The board may specify the duties of and in accordance with this by-law and the law, delegate to such officers powers to manage the business and affairs of the Corporation.

7.02 **Chairman of the Board:** The chairman of the board shall, when present, preside at all meetings of the board of directors, committees of directors and, in the absence of the president, at all meetings of shareholders. In addition, the board may assign to him any of the powers and duties that may by the provisions of this by-law be assigned to the managing director or to the president; and he shall have such other powers and duties as the board may specify.

7.03 Managing Director: The managing director, if any shall be a resident Canadian, and exercise such powers and have such authority as may be delegated to him by the board of directors in accordance with the provisions of Section 110 of the Act and, in particular, the board may delegate to him such of the powers and duties as may be assigned by this by-law to a general manager or manager.

7.04 President:

    (i)   The board, from time to time, may elect from among its number, a President.

    (ii)   The President shall be the chief executive officer of the corporation, and preside at all General Meetings and, in the absence or non-appointment of the Chairman of the Board, shall also preside at meetings of the Board. He shall have general and active management of the business and affairs of the Corporation, and without limitation to the foregoing:

        (1)   he shall have general superintendence and direction of all the other officers of the Corporation;

        (2)   he shall submit the annual report of the board, if any, and the annual balance sheets and financial statements of the business and affairs and reports on the financial position of the Corporation as required by the Statutes to the Annual General Meeting and from time to time he shall report to the board of all matters within his knowledge which the interest of the Corporation requires to be brought to their attention;

        (3)   he shall be ex-officio a member of all standing committees.

7.05 Vice-President: During the absence or disability of the president, his duties shall be performed and his powers exercised by the vice-president or, if there are more than one, by the vice-president designated from time to time by the board for the president; provided, however, that a vice-president who is not a director shall not preside as chairman at any meeting of directors or of a committee of directors. A vice-president shall have such other powers and duties as the board or the president may prescribe.

7.06 Secretary: The secretary or if none is appointed, the President, shall attend and be the secretary of all meetings of the board, shareholders and committees of the board and shall enter or cause to be entered in records kept for that purpose minutes of all proceedings thereat; he shall give or cause to be given, as and when instructed, all notices to shareholders, directors, officers, auditors and members of committees of the board; he shall be the custodian of the stamp or mechanical device generally used for affixing the corporate seal of the Corporation and of all books, papers, records, documents and instruments belonging to the Corporation, except when some other officer or agent has been appointed for that purpose; and he shall have such other powers and duties as the board or the chief executive officer may specify.

7.07 Treasurer: The treasurer shall keep proper accounting records in compliance with the Act and shall be responsible for the deposit of money, the safekeeping of the securities and the disbursement of funds of the Corporation; he shall render to the board whenever required an account of all his transactions and he shall have such other powers and duties as the board or the chief executive officer may specify.

7.08 General Manager or Manager: If elected or appointed, the general manager shall have, subject to the authority of the board, the manager director, if any, and the president, full power to manage and direct the business and affairs of the Corporation (except such matters and duties as by law must be transacted or performed by the board of directors and/or by the shareholders) and to employ and discharge agents and employees of the Corporation or may delegate to him or them any lesser authority. A general manager or manager shall conform to all lawful orders given to him by the board of directors of the Corporation and shall at all reasonable times give to the directors or any of them all information they may require regarding the affairs of the Corporation. Any agent or employee appointed by a general manager or manager shall be subject to discharge by the board of directors.

7.09 Powers and Duties of Other Officers: The powers and duties of all other officers shall be such as the terms of their engagement call for or as the board, the managing director, or the President may specify. Any of the powers and duties of an officer to whom an assistant has been appointed may be exercised and performed by such assistant, unless the board or the chief executive officer otherwise directs.

7.10 Variation of Powers and Duties: The board may from time to time and subject to the provisions of the Act, vary, add to, or limit the powers and duties of any officer.

7.11 Term of Office: The board, in its discretion, may remove any officer of the Corporation, without prejudice to such officer's rights under any employment contract. Otherwise each officer appointed by the board shall hold office until his successor is appointed, or until his earlier resignation.

7.12 **Vacancies:** If the office of any officer of the Corporation shall be or become vacant by reason of death, resignation, disqualification or otherwise, the directors by resolution shall, in the case of the president or the secretary, and may, in the case of any other office, appoint a person to fill such vacancy.

7.13 **Remuneration and Removal:** The remuneration of all officers appointed by the board of directors shall be determined from time to time by resolution of the board of directors. The fact that any officer or employee is a director or shareholder of the Corporation shall not disqualify him from receiving such remuneration as may be determined. All officers, in the absence of agreement to the contrary, shall be subject to removal by resolution of the board of directors at any time, with or without cause.

7.14 **Agents and Attorneys:** The Corporation, by or under the authority of the board, shall have power from time to time to appoint agents or attorneys for the Corporation in or outside Canada with such powers (including the power to sub-delegate) of management, administration or otherwise as may be thought fit.

7.15 **Conflict of Interest:** An officer shall disclose his interest in any material contract or proposed material contract with the Corporation.

7.16 **Fidelity Bonds:** The board may require such officers, employees and agents of the Corporation as the board deems advisable to furnish bonds for the faithful discharge of their powers and duties, in such forms and with such surety as the board may from time to time determine.

7.17 **Executive Committee:**

    (a)   Whenever the number of directors constituting the board shall consist of more than six (6), the board may appoint not less than three (3) of their number to constitute an Executive Committee, of whom a majority shall constitute a quorum, and who may meet at stated times or on notice to all or any of their own number; the members of such Committee shall advise with and aid the officers and the board in all matters concerning the Corporation's interests and in the management of its business and affairs and generally perform such duties and exercise such powers as may be directed or delegated to such Committee by the board from time to time. The board may delegate to such Committee authority to exercise such of its powers while the board is not in session as the board may designate. Unless and until the board otherwise determines, the president and any directors elected by the board shall constitute the Executive Committee of the Corporation and shall be and are hereby vested with authority to exercise all of the powers of the board while such board is not in session, except such powers as the Statutes are required to be exercised by the board.

    (b)   The Executive Committee may act by the written consent of a quorum thereof, although not formally convened.

    (c)   The Executive Committee shall keep minutes of its proceedings and report the same to the board at the next meeting thereof.

    (d)   A majority of the Executive Committee shall be Canadian residents.

Division Eight
SHAREHOLDERS' MEETINGS

8.01 **Annual Meetings:** Subject to Section 127 of the Act, the annual meeting of shareholders shall be held at such time and on such day in each year and, subject to Section 8.03, at such place or places as the board, the chairman of the board, the managing director or the president may from time to time determine, for the purpose of considering the financial statements and reports required by the Act to be placed before the annual meeting, elected directors, appointing an auditor if required by the Act or the articles, and for the transaction of such other business as may properly be brought before the meeting.

8.02 **Special Meetings:** The board, the chairman of the board, the managing director or the president shall have the power to call a special meeting of shareholders at any time. A special meeting may also be called by any shareholder or director on the refusal or inability of the above to call one, provided the caller of the meeting bears all of the expenses of calling and holding the meeting.

8.03 **Place of Meetings:** Meetings of shareholders shall be held at any place within Alberta as the directors may by resolution determine or, if all the shareholders entitled to vote at the meeting so agree or if the articles so provide, outside Alberta.

8.04 **Record Date for Notice:** The board may fix in advance a date, preceding the date of any meeting of shareholders by not more than 50 days and not less than 21 days, as a record for the determination of shareholders entitled to notice of the meeting. If no record date is fixed, the record date for the determination of the shareholders entitled to receive notice of the meeting shall be the close of business on the date immediately preceding the day on which the notice is given or, if no notice is given, the day on which the meeting is held.

8.05   Notice: A printed, written or typewritten notice stating the day, hour and place of each meeting of shareholders shall be given in the manner provided in Section 13.01 not less than 7 nor more than 30 days before the date of the meeting to each director, to the auditor, and to each shareholder who at the close of business on the record date for notice is entered in the securities register as the holder of one or more shares carrying the right to vote at the meeting. Notice of a meeting of shareholders called for any purpose other than consideration of the financial statements and auditor's report, election of directors and re-appointment of the incumbent auditor shall state the nature of such business in sufficient detail to permit the shareholders to form a reasoned judgment thereon and shall state the text of any special resolution to be submitted to the meeting.

8.06   Right to Vote: At any meeting of shareholders, every person shall be entitled to vote who, on the record date, or if no record date is set, at the close of business on the date preceding the date notice is sent, or if no notice is sent, on the date of the meeting, is entered in the securities register as the holder of one or more shares carrying the right to vote at such meeting, except:

(a)   that where such person transfers his shares after the record date is set, or if no record date is set, after the close of business on the date preceding the date notice of the meeting is sent to shareholders and

(b)   the transferee, at least 10 days prior to the meeting, produces properly endorsed share certificates to the secretary or transfer agent of the Corporation or otherwise establishes his ownership of the share

in which case the transferee may vote those shares. If notice is not sent, the transferee may establish his ownership to the shares in the manner aforesaid at any time prior to the holding of the meeting.

8.07   Waiver of Notice: A shareholder and any other person entitled to attend a meeting of shareholders may in any manner waive notice of a meeting of shareholders and attendance of any such person at a meeting of shareholders shall constitute a waiver of notice of the meeting except where such person attends a meeting for the express purpose of objecting to the transaction of any business on the grounds that the meeting is not lawfully called.

8.08   Chairman, Secretary and Scrutineers: The president or, in his absence, the chairman of the board, if such an officer has been elected or appointed and is present, otherwise a vice-president who is a shareholder of the Corporation shall be chairman of any meeting of shareholders. If no such officer is present within 15 minutes from the time fixed for holding the meeting, the persons present and those entitled to vote shall choose one of their number to be chairman. If the secretary of the Corporation is absent, the chairman shall appoint some person, who need not be a shareholder, to act as secretary of the meeting, if desired, one or more scrutineers, who need not be shareholders, may be appointed by a resolution or by the chairman with the consent of the Meeting.

8.09   Persons Entitled to be Present: The only persons entitled to be present at a meeting of shareholders shall be those entitled to vote thereat, the directors and auditors of the Corporation and others who, although not entitled to vote, are entitled or required under any provision of the Act or the articles or by-laws to be present at the meeting. Any other person may be admitted only on the invitation of the chairman of the meeting or with the consent of the meeting.

8.10   Quorum: Subject to the Act, a quorum for the transaction of business at any meeting of shareholders shall be _____persons present in person, each being a shareholder entitled to vote thereat or a duly appointed proxyholder or representative for a shareholder so entitled. If a quorum is present at the opening of any meeting of shareholders, the shareholders present or represented may proceed with the business of the meeting notwithstanding that a quorum is not present throughout the meeting. If a quorum is not present at the opening of the meeting of shareholders, the shareholders present or represented may adjourn the meeting to a fixed time and place but may not transact any other business. If a meeting is so adjourned to a fixed time and place, then any members present shall then constitute a quorum.

8.11   Participation in Meeting by Telephone: A shareholder or any other person entitled to attend a meeting of shareholders may participate in the meeting by means of telephone or other telecommunication facilities that permit all persons participating in the meeting to hear each other (if all the shareholders entitled to vote at the meeting consent) and a person participating in such a meeting by those means is deemed to be present at the meeting.

8.12   Proxyholders and Representatives: Votes at meetings of the shareholders may be given either personally or by proxy; or, in the case of a shareholder who is a body corporate or association, by an individual authorized by a resolution of the board of directors or governing body of the body corporate or association to represent it at a meeting of shareholders of the Corporation, upon producing a certified copy of such resolution or otherwise establishing his authority to vote to the satisfaction of the secretary or the chairman.

A proxy shall be executed by the shareholder or his attorney authorized in writing and is valid only at the meeting in respect to which it is given or any adjournment of that meeting. A person appointed by proxy need not be a shareholder.

SELF-COUNSEL PRESS–CDN-INC-ALT (4-10)01

Subject to the regulations, a proxy may be in the following form:

The undersigned shareholder of **TABLE TRAPPINGS DESIGN & MANUFACTURE INC.**_____

hereby appoints_____ of_____

or failing him,_____ as the nominee of the undersigned to attend and act for the

undersigned and on behalf of the undersigned at the_____

meeting of the shareholders of the said Corporation to be held on the_____ day of_____. 20____ and at any

adjournment or adjournments thereof.

DATED this_____ day of_____, 20____

_____
Signature of Shareholder

8.13   Time for Deposit of Proxies: The board may specify in a notice calling a meeting of shareholders a time, preceding the time of such meeting by not more than 48 hours exclusive of Saturdays and holidays, before which time proxies to be used at such meeting must be deposited. A proxy shall be acted upon only if, prior to the time so specified, it shall have been deposited with the Corporation or an agent thereof specified in such notice or if, no such time having been specified in such notice, it has been received by the secretary of the Corporation or by the chairman of the meeting or any adjournment thereof prior to the time of voting.

8.14   Validity Following Death or Transfer: A vote given in accordance with the terms of a proxy shall be valid notwithstanding the previous death of the principal or transfer of the share with respect to which the vote is given, provided notice in writing of such death or transfer shall not have been received by the Corporation at least 24 hours before the meeting at the place at which the proxies are to be deposited, nor by the chairman of the meeting at the time of the holding of the meeting.

8.15   Joint Shareholders: If two or more persons hold shares jointly, any one of them present in person or duly represented at a meeting of shareholders may, in the absence of the other or others, vote the shares; but if two or more of those persons are present in person or represented and vote, they shall vote as one the shares jointly held by them. If they cannot or do not agree on the vote of their joint holdings then their vote shall not be taken.

8.16   Votes to Govern: At any meeting of shareholders every question shall, unless otherwise required by the articles or by-laws or by-law, be determined by a majority of the votes cast on the question. In case of an equality of votes either upon a show of hands or upon a ballot, the chairman of the meeting shall be entitled to a second or casting vote.

8.17   Show of Hands: Subject to the Act, any question at a meeting of shareholders shall be decided by a show of hands, unless a ballot thereon is required or demanded as hereinafter provided. Upon a show of hands every person who is present and entitled to vote shall have one vote. Whenever a vote by show of hands shall have been taken upon a question, unless a ballot thereon is so required or demanded, a declaration by the chairman of the meeting that the vote upon the question has been carried or carried by a particular majority or not carried and an entry to that effect in the minutes of the meeting shall be prima facie evidence of the fact without proof of the number of the votes recorded in favor or against any resolution or other proceeding in respect of the said question, and the result of the vote so taken shall be the decision of shareholders upon the said question.

8.18   Ballots: On any question proposed for consideration at a meeting of shareholders, a shareholder, proxyholder or other person entitled to vote may demand and the chairman may require that a ballot be taken either before or upon the declaration of the result of any vote by show of hands. If a ballot is demanded on the election of a chairman or on the question of an adjournment it shall be taken forthwith without an adjournment. A ballot demanded or required on any other question shall be taken in such manner as the chairman shall direct. A demand or requirement for a ballot may be withdrawn at any time prior to the taking of the ballot. If a ballot is taken each person present shall be entitled, in respect to the shares that he is entitled to vote at the meeting upon the question, to the number of votes as provided for by the articles or, in the absence of such provision in the articles, to one vote for each share he is entitled to vote. The result of the ballot so taken shall be the decision of the shareholders upon the question.

8.19   Adjournment: The chairman at a meeting of shareholders may, with the consent of the meeting and subject to such conditions as the meeting may decide, adjourn the meeting from time to time and from place to place. If a meeting of shareholders is adjourned for less than 30 days, it shall not be necessary to give notice of the adjourned meeting, other than by announcement at the time of the adjournment. Subject to the Act, if a meeting of shareholders is adjourned by one or more adjournments for an aggregate of 30 days or more, notice of the adjourned meeting shall be given in the same manner as notice for an original meeting.

SELF-COUNSEL PRESS–CDN-INC-ALT (4-11)01

8.20   Resolution in Lieu of a Meeting: Notwithstanding any of the foregoing provisions of this by-law a resolution in writing either ordinary or special signed by all the shareholders entitled to vote on that resolution at a meeting of shareholders is as valid as if it had been passed at a meeting of the shareholders.

8.21   Only One Shareholder: Where the Corporation has only one shareholder or only one holder of any class or series of shares, that shareholder present in person or duly represented constitutes a meeting.

Division Nine

SHARES

9.01   Allotment and Issuance: Subject to Section 25 of the Act, the articles and any unanimous shareholder agreement, the board may from time to time allot or grant options to purchase the whole or any part, including fractional parts of the authorized and unissued shares of the Corporation at such times and to such persons and for such consideration as the board shall determine, provided that no share shall be issued until it is fully paid as provided by the Act.

9.02   Commissions: The board may from time to time authorize the Corporation to pay a reasonable commission to any person in consideration of his purchasing or agreeing to purchase shares of the Corporation, whether from the Corporation or from any other person, or procuring or agreeing to procure purchasers for any such shares.

9.03   Non-Recognition of Trusts: Subject to the Act, the Corporation may treat the registered holder of any share as the person exclusively entitled to vote, to receive notices, to receive any dividend or other payments in respect of the share, and otherwise to exercise all the rights and powers of an owner of the share.

9.04   Certificates: Share certificates and the form of stock transfer power on the reverse side thereof shall (subject to the Provisions of the Act) be in such form as the board of directors may by resolution approve and such certificates shall be signed manually by the chairman of the board, or the president, or the vice-president, or the secretary, or by on behalf of a registrar, transfer agent or branch transfer agent of the Corporation, if any. The corporate seal, if any, need not be impressed upon a share certificate issued by the Corporation.

9.05   Replacement of Share Certificates: The board or any officer or agent designated by the board may in its or his discretion direct the issue of a new share or other such certificate in lieu of and upon cancellation of a certificate that has been mutilated or in substitution for a certificate claimed to have been lost, destroyed or wrongfully taken on payment of such reasonable fee and on such terms as to indemnity, reimbursement of expenses and evidence of loss and of title as the board may from time to time prescribe, whether generally or in any particular case.

9.06   Joint Holders: If two or more persons are registered as joint holders of any share, the Corporation shall not be bound to issue more than one certificate in respect thereof, and delivery of such certificate to one of such persons shall be sufficient to all of them. Any one of such persons may give effectual receipts for the certificate issued in respect thereof or for any dividend, bonus, return of capital or other money payable or warrant issuable in respect of such share.

Division Ten

TRANSFER OF SECURITIES

10.01 Registration of Transfer: Subject to the Act, no transfer of a share shall be registered in a securities register except upon presentation of the certificate representing such share with an endorsement which complies with the Act made thereon or delivered therewith duly executed by an appropriate person as provided by the Act, together with such reasonable assurance that the endorsement is genuine and effective as the board may from time to time prescribe, upon payment of all applicable taxes and any reasonable fees prescribed by the board and upon compliance with such restrictions on transfer as are authorized by the articles and upon satisfaction of any lien referred to in Section 10.04.

10.02 Transfer Agents and Registrars: The board may from time to time by resolution appoint or remove one or more transfer agents registered under the Trust Companies Act to maintain a central securities register or registers and one or more branch transfer agents to maintain branch securities register or registers. A transfer agent or branch transfer agent so appointed may be designated as such or may be designated as a registrar, according to his functions, and a person may be appointed and designed with the functions of both registrar and transfer or branch transfer agent. The board may provide for the registration of transfers of securities by and in the offices of such transfer, or branch transfer agents or registrars. In the event of any such appointment in respect of any of the shares of the Corporation, all share certificates issued by the Corporation in respect to those shares shall be countersigned by on behalf of one of the said transfer agents, branch transfer agents or registrars, if any, as the case may be.

SELF-COUNSEL PRESS–CDN-INC-ALT (4-12)01

10.03 Securities Registers: A central securities register of the Corporation shall be kept at the designated records office of the Corporation, if any, otherwise the registered office of the Corporation, or at an office or offices of a corporation or corporations registered under the Trust Companies Act as may from time to time be designated by resolution of the board of directors to act as the Corporation's transfer agent or agents. Branch securities register or registers may be kept either in or outside Alberta at such office or offices of the Corporation as the directors may determine, or at the office or offices of such other person or persons or corporations as may from time to time be designated by the resolution of the directors to act as the Corporation's branch transfer agent or agents. A branch securities register shall contain particulars of securities issued or transferred at that branch. Particulars of each issue or transfer of a security registered in a branch securities register shall also be kept in the corresponding central securities register.

10.04 Deceased Shareholders: In the event of the death of a holder, or of one of the joint holders, of any share, the Corporation shall not be required to make any entry in the securities register in respect thereof or to make any dividend or other payments in respect thereof except upon production of all such documents as may be required by law and upon compliance with the reasonable requirements of the Corporation and its transfer agents.

10.05 Lien for Indebtedness: If the articles provide that the Corporation shall have a lien on shares registered in the name of a shareholder indebted to the Corporation for any unpaid amount owing on a share issued by the Corporation on the date the Corporation was continued under the Act, such lien may be enforced, subject to the articles and to any unanimous shareholder agreement, by the sale of the shares thereby affected or by any other action, suit, remedy or proceeding authorized or permitted by law or by equity and, pending such enforcement, the Corporation may refuse to register a transfer of the whole or any part of such shares.

10.06 Alteration of share capital: Subject to the provisions of the Act, the Corporation may, by resolution of the board or of the members:

    (a)   increase the maximum price or consideration for which shares without nominal or par value may be issued, where such maximum price or consideration has been stated in the articles;

    (b)   cancel shares which, at the date of the passing of the above-mentioned resolution, have not been taken or agreed to be taken by any person, and diminish the amount of its share capital by the number of shares cancelled;

    (c)   cancel paid-up shares which are surrendered to the Corporation by way of gift and, if the resolution so provides, diminish the amount of its share capital by the number of shares cancelled;

    (d)   cancel paid-up shares that are acquired by the Corporation on a distribution of the assets of another company under liquidation proceedings, and, if the resolution so provides, diminish the amount of its share capital by the number of shares cancelled.

Division Eleven

DIVIDENDS AND RIGHTS

11.01 Dividends: Subject to the Act, the board may from time to time declare dividends payable to the shareholders according to their respective rights and interest in the Corporation. Dividends may be paid in money or property or by issuing fully paid shares of the Corporation.

11.02 Dividend Cheques: A dividend payable in money shall be paid by cheque to the order of each registered holder of shares of the class or series in respect of which it has been declared, and mailed by prepaid ordinary mail to such registered holder at his address recorded in the Corporation's securities register or registers unless such holder otherwise directs. In the case of joint holders the cheque shall, unless such joint holders otherwise direct, be made payable to the order of all such joint holders and mailed to them at their recorded address. The mailing of such cheque as aforesaid, unless the same is not paid on due presentation, shall satisfy and discharge the liability for the dividend to the extent of the sum represented thereby plus the amount of any tax which the Corporation is required to and does withhold.

11.03 Non-Receipt of Cheques: In the event of non-receipt of any dividend cheque by the person to whom it is sent as aforesaid, the Corporation shall issue to such person a replacement cheque for a like amount on such terms as to indemnity, reimbursement of expenses and evidence of non-receipt and of title as the board may from time to time prescribe, whether generally or in any particular case.

11.04 Unclaimed Dividends: Any dividend unclaimed after a period of 2 years from the date of which the same has been declared to be payable shall be forfeited and shall revert to the Corporation.

SELF-COUNSEL PRESS–CDN-INC-ALT (4-13)01

11.05 Record Date for Dividends and Rights: The board may fix in advance a date, preceding by not more than 50 days the date for the payment of any dividend or the date for the issue of any warrant or other evidence of the right to subscribe for securities of the Corporation, as a record date for the determination of the persons entitled to receive payment of such dividend or to exercise the right to subscribe for such securities, and notice of any such record date shall be given not less than 7 days before such record date in the manner provided by the Act. If no record date is so fixed, the record date for the determination of the persons entitled to receive payment of any dividend or to exercise the right to subscribe for securities of the Corporation shall be at the close of business on the day on which the resolution relating to such dividend or right to subscribe is passed by the board.

11.06 Deduction from Dividends Payable: The Corporation may deduct from the dividends payable to any member all such sums of money as may be due from him to the Corporation on account of debts, obligations or otherwise.

Division Twelve

INFORMATION AVAILABLE TO SHAREHOLDERS

12.01 Except as provided by the Act and in paragraph 12.02 no shareholder shall be entitled to obtain information respecting any details or conduct of the Corporation's business which in the opinion of the directors would be inexpedient in the interests of the Corporation to communicate to the public.

12.02 The directors may from time to time, subject to rights conferred by the Act, determine whether and to what extent and at what time and place and under what conditions or regulations the documents, books and registers and accounting records of the Corporation or any of them shall be open to the inspection of shareholders and no shareholder shall have any right to inspect any document or book or register or account record of the Corporation except as conferred by statute or authorized by the board of directors or by a resolution of the shareholders.

Division Thirteen

NOTICES

13.01 Method of Giving Notices: Any notice or other document required by the Act, the Regulations, the articles or the by-laws to be sent to any shareholder or director or to the auditor shall be delivered personally or sent by prepaid mail or by telegram or cable or telex to any such shareholder at his latest address as shown in the records of the Corporation or its transfer agent and to any such director at his latest address as shown in the records of the Corporation or in the last notice filed under Section 101 or 108 of the Act, and to the auditor at his business address. A notice shall be deemed to be given when it is delivered personally to any such person or to his address as aforesaid; a notice mailed shall be deemed to have been given when deposited in a post office or public letter box; and a notice sent by any means of transmitted or recorded communication shall be deemed to have been given when dispatched or delivered to the appropriate communication company or agency or its representative for dispatch. The secretary may change or cause to be changed the recorded address of any shareholder, director, officer, auditor or member of a committee of the board in accordance with any information believed by him to be reliable.

13.02 Notice to Joint Shareholders: If two or more persons are registered as joint holders of any share, any notice may be addressed to all of such joint holders but notice addressed to one of such persons shall be sufficient notice to all of them.

13.03 Persons Entitled by Death or Operation of Law: Every person who, by operation of law, transfer, death of a shareholder or any other means whatsoever, shall become entitled to any share, shall be bound by every notice in respect of such share which shall have been duly given to the shareholder from whom he derives his title to such share prior to his name and address being entered on the securities register (whether such notice was given before or after the happening of the event upon which he became so entitled) and prior to his furnishing to the Corporation the proof of authority or evidence of his entitlement prescribed by the Act.

13.04 Non-Receipt of Notices: If a notice or document is sent to a shareholder by prepaid mail in accordance with Section 13.01 and the notice or document is returned on two consecutive occasions, it shall not be necessary to send any further notice or document to the shareholder until he informs the Corporation in writing of his new address; provided, always, that the return of a notice of a shareholders' meeting mailed to a shareholder in accordance with Section 13.01 of this by-law shall be deemed to be received by the shareholder on the date deposited in the mail notwithstanding the return of the notice.

13.05 Ommissions and Errors: The accidental omission to give any notice to any shareholder, director, officer, auditor or member of a committee of the board or the non-receipt of any notice by any such person or any error in any notice not affecting the substance thereof shall not invalidate any action taken at any meeting held pursuant to such notice or otherwise founded thereon.

SELF-COUNSEL PRESS–CDN-INC-ALT (4-14)01

13.06 Signature on Notices: Unless otherwise specifically provided, the signature of any director or officer of the Corporation to any notice or document to be given by the Corporation may be written, stamped, typewritten or printed or partly written, stamped, typewritten or printed.

13.07 Waiver of Notice: Any shareholder, proxyholder, other person entitled to attend a meeting of shareholders, director, officer, auditor or member of a committee of the board may at any time waive any notice, or waive or abridge the time for any notice, required to be given to him under the Act, the Regulations thereunder, the articles, the by-laws or otherwise and such waiver or abridgement, whether given before or after the meeting or other event of which notice is required to be given, shall cure any default in the giving or in the time of such notice, as the case may be. Any such waiver or abridgement shall be in writing except a waiver of notice of a meeting of shareholders or of the board of a committee of the board which may be given in any manner.

13.08 Certification of Notice: A certificate of a duly authorized person as to the facts in relation to the giving of any notice shall be prima facie evidence thereof.

13.09 Computation of Time: In computing the date when notice must be given under any provision requiring a specified number of days notice of any meeting or other event, the date of giving of the notice shall be excluded and the date of the meeting or other event shall be included.

Division Fourteen

MISCELLANEOUS

14.01 Financial Year: Until changed by the board, the financial year of the Corporation shall end on the last day of _____DECEMBER_____ in each year.

14.02 Directors to Require Surrender of Share Certificates: The directors in office when the Certificate of Continuance is issued under the Act are hereby authorized to require the shareholders of the Corporation to surrender their share certificates, or such of their share certificates as the directors may determine, for the purpose of cancelling the share certificates and replacing them with new share certificates that comply with the Act, in particular, replacing existing share certificates with share certificates that are not negotiable securities under the Act. The directors in office shall act by resolution under this section and shall in their discretion decide the manner in which they shall require the surrender of existing share certificates and the time within which the shareholders must comply with the requirement and the form or forms of the share certificates to be issued in place of the existing share certificates. The directors may take such proceedings as they deem necessary to compel any shareholder to comply with a requirement to surrender his share certificate or certificates pursuant to this section. Notwithstanding any other provision of this by-law, but subject to the Act, the directors may refuse to register the transfer of shares represented by a share certificate that has not been surrendered pursuant to a requirement under this section.

14.03 Shareholders' Approval to Amend By-Law No. 1: The directors shall not, without the prior approval of the shareholders entitled to vote at an annual meeting of the Corporation, given by ordinary resolution, amend or repeal any provision of this by-law.

14.04 Effective Date: This by-law shall come into force upon the issue of the Certificate of Incorporation under the Act.

14.05 Unanimous Shareholder Agreement: The provisions of the by-laws shall in all respects be subject to the terms of any unanimous shareholder agreement and every director and officer shall comply therewith, and a notice thereof shall be conspicuously placed on every certificate for shares in the Corporation,

ENACTED this __1ST__ day of __JANUARY__, 20_01_.

_____*Sally Smith*_____   _____*Mary Jones*_____
President   Secretary

SAMPLE 10
SAMPLE SHARE CERTIFICATE

"ITEM B"

Company

SHARE CERTIFICATE

TRANSFER DETAILS

Certificate # _____ Class _____ No. of Shares _____

Registered Name _____

Date entered in

Register of Members _____ 20 _____

From: _____

To: _____

Received (Certificate Number) _____

this _____ day of _____, 20 _____

_____ **SHARES**

NO: _____

INCORPORATED UNDER THE LAW OF THE PROVINCE OF ALBERTA

This is to certify that _____

is the registered holder of _____, Class: _____

fully paid and non-assessable shares of _____

without par value

Restrictions on Transfer. There are restrictions on the right to transfer the said shares and a copy of the full text thereof is obtainable on demand and without fee from the Corporation.

IN WITNESS WHEREOF, the Corporation has caused this certificate to be signed by its duly

Authorized officer(s) this _____ **day of** _____ **20** _____

_____

1.1c   Adopt Corporate Seal

Under current Alberta law, corporate seals are no longer required. The authorized signing officers for the corporation can sign documents without a seal, and those documents are legally binding.

However, the idea of the seal has not disappeared. Banks like to see seals on corporate documents relating to loans, and the Alberta land titles system still recognizes a seal on documents relating to ownership of land. Mary and Sally are going to get a seal, just in case. They will make an impression of it on the minutes of the organizational meeting of first directors to show that it is the official seal of their corporation.

1.1d   Appoint Officers

Since Sally started the business herself, she is going to be President, and Mary will be Secretary Treasurer. This is significant because according to By-law No. 1, the president is automatically the chair of both the directors' and shareholders' meetings. That means Sally gets the casting vote, which gives her power over all corporate decisions.

1.1e   Issue Shares to Shareholders

The first directors issue the first shares, and those shareholders then get power to elect the directors of the corporation. Most corporations the size of Sally and Mary's do not actually give the share certificates to the shareholders. This makes sense because shares in non-distributing corporations cannot be sold to other members of the public, and that condition was included in the articles of incorporation of this corporation. Instead, the certificates are kept in the minute book, which will be discussed in section **1.3**.

1.1f   Authorize Banking

Even though this part of the minutes gives the corporate officers full authority to do any necessary banking for the corporation, and even though that power is also spelled out in detail in Section 2 of By-Law No. 1, many banks have their own banking forms that they want the corporation to sign. If so, these forms should be attached to these minutes.

1.1g   Dispense with Appointment of Auditor

A full-scale audit of the corporation's books is an expensive affair, but a very necessary one when the shareholders are not involved in the daily operations of the corporation. Without an audit, the shareholders will never know how the corporation is doing financially.

But the shareholders of a small corporation like this one are actively involved in the activities of the corporation and have all its financial information at their fingertips. For that reason, they do not want to pay for an annual audit.

Instead of appointing an auditor for the corporation, Mary and Sally are appointing an accountant to give it financial advice and to look after preparation and filing of the annual profit-and-loss statement and tax returns.

1.1h Waiver of Notice of the Meeting

Here, Mary and Sally are saying that they don't need formal, advance, written notice of this meeting as set out in the law, and they are invoking the sections in the by-law that permit waiver of formal notice.

1.2 First meeting of shareholders

The first directors have done all the work necessary in their first meeting, so all the shareholders have to do is accept what was done and elect directors to hold office until the annual meeting. As you can see from the sample minutes of the shareholders' meeting, included here as Sample 11, these minutes are quite short. The first meeting of shareholders usually takes care of the following items:

1.2a Elect Directors

Once the job of the first directors is done, they no longer hold office, so the shareholders must now elect new ones. Of course there is no surprise. Shareholders Mary and Sally are going to elect Mary and Sally as directors.

1.2b Confirm Bylaw 1

The law requires that the shareholders confirm and adopt any by-laws that were adopted by the directors.

1.2c Confirm Decision Not to Appoint Auditor

As said above, an auditor is appointed for the protection of the shareholders, so they must confirm the directors' decision not to appoint one.

1.3 Setting up the minute book

Once these meetings are over, the directors must put the paper away where it can be found when needed for future reference. The usual way

Minutes of the First Meeting of Shareholders

Minutes of the First Meeting of the Shareholders of___TABLE TRAPPINGS DESIGN &___,
_____MANUFACTURE INC._____

held at___EDMONTON___, Alberta, on the__10th__ day of_____JUNE_____ 20_01_.

_____SALLY SMITH AND MARY JONES_____, the shareholders of the corporation,
were present and passed the following resolutions:

1) _____SALLY SMITH AND MARY JONES_____ were appointed directors
of the corporation until further notice.

2) The adoption of By-law Number 1 was confirmed.

3) The shareholders agreed that the corporation not appoint an auditor and that_____
_____BILL ROY_____ be appointed accountant for the corporation.

4) By signing this minute, the shareholders waive formal notice of this meeting and ratify all
business transacted.

There being no further business, the meeting was adjourned.

_____Sally Smith_____

_____Mary Jones_____

to store corporate papers is in a three-ring binder called a minute book, and this book is kept at the corporate records address.

Minute books can be bought from stationery and office-supply stores. They are also available from Self-Counsel Press. Minute books come complete with pre-printed, labelled dividers.

The minute book for Sally and Mary's corporation will need dividers for the following documents:

- Certificate of Incorporation

- Articles of Incorporation

- By-laws

- Notice of Address

- Notice of Directors

- Register of Directors

- Register of Shareholders

- Share Certificates

- Minutes of Directors' Meetings

- Minutes of Shareholders' Meetings

- Particulars of Share Transfers

- Register of Mortgages

- Annual Returns

The first five documents have already been discussed. The next three — the register of directors, the register of shareholders, and the share certificates — have been completed for Sally and Mary's company and are included here as Sample 12, Sample 13, and Sample 14, respectively.

The Particulars of Share Transfers (Sample 15) is blank because neither Mary nor Sally have yet had to ask the directors for permission to sell their shares to someone else. Similarly, the Register of Mortgages (Sample 16) is blank because the corporation has not taken out any mortgages.

Finally, there is nothing in the Annual Returns section, yet. The corporation won't file its first annual return for a year, and that process is discussed in section **6.2**.

REGISTER OF DIRECTORS AND OFFICERS

Register of Directors and Officers of   TABLE TRAPPINGS DESIGN & MANUFACTURE INC.

Full Name	Address	Occupation	Date When Appointed or Elected	Date When Ceased to Hold Office	Position Held
SALLY SMITH	12345 67 AVE. EDMONTON AB A1B 2C3	BUSINESS PERSON	10 JANUARY 2001		PRESIDENT
MARY JONES	12347 67 AVE. EDMONTON AB A1B 2C3	BUSINESS PERSON	10 JANUARY 2001		SECRETARY TREASURER

REGISTER OF SHAREHOLDERS (MEMBERS)

REGISTER OF MEMBERS

Register of Members of ___TABLE TRAPPINGS DESIGN & MANUFACTURE INC.___

Full Name	Address	Occupation	Date When Entered as a Member	Date When Ceased to be a Member	Representative Capacity (if any)
SALLY SMITH	12345 67 AVE. EDMONTON AB A1B 2C3	BUSINESS PERSON	10 JANUARY 2001		
MARY JONES	12347 67 AVE. EDMONTON AB A1B 2C3	BUSINESS PERSON	10 JANUARY 2001		

SAMPLE 14
COMPLETED SHARE CERTIFICATES

Company TABLE TRAPPINGS DESIGN & MANUFACTURE INC.

SHARE CERTIFICATE

Certificate # 1   Class A   No. of Shares 100
Registered Name SALLY SMITH
Date entered in
Register of Members JANUARY 10   20 01

TRANSFER DETAILS

From:
To:
Received (Certificate Number)
this   day of   , 20

NO: 1

TABLE TRAPPINGS DESIGN & MANUFACTURE INC.
INCORPORATED UNDER THE LAW OF THE PROVINCE OF ALBERTA

100   **SHARES**

This is to certify that SALLY SMITH
is the registered holder of 100   , Class: A
fully paid and non-assessable shares of TABLE TRAPPINGS DESIGN & MANUFACTURE INC.

without par value

Restrictions on Transfer. *There are restrictions on the right to transfer the said shares and a copy of the full text thereof is obtainable on demand and without fee from the Corporation.*

IN WITNESS WHEREOF, the Corporation has caused this certificate to be signed by its duly
Authorized officer(s) this 10th **day of** JANUARY **20** 01

Sally Smith   *Mary Jones*

Company TABLE TRAPPINGS DESIGN & MANUFACTURE INC.

SHARE CERTIFICATE   **TRANSFER DETAILS**

Certificate # 2   Class A   No. of Shares 100

Registered Name MARY JONES

Date entered in

Register of Members JANUARY 10   20 01

From:

To:

Received (Certificate Number)

this   day of   , 20

NO: 2

100 SHARES

TABLE TRAPPINGS DESIGN & MANUFACTURE INC.

INCORPORATED UNDER THE LAW OF THE PROVINCE OF ALBERTA

This is to certify that MARY JONES

is the registered holder of 100   , Class: A

fully paid and non-assessable shares of TABLE TRAPPINGS DESIGN & MANUFACTURE INC.

without par value

Restrictions on Transfer. *There are restrictions on the right to transfer the said shares and a copy of the full text thereof is obtainable on demand and without fee from the Corporation.*

IN WITNESS WHEREOF, the Corporation has caused this certificate to be signed by its duly

Authorized officer(s) this 10th   day of   JANUARY   20 01

Sally Smith   *Mary Jones*

PARTICULARS OF SHARE TRANSFERS

Particulars of Share Transfers of_____

No. of Transfer	Date	Class of Share	Certificate Surrendered		Name of Transferor	Name of Transferee	Address	Certificate Issued		Signature of Transferor or Attorney
			Number	Shares				Number	Shares	

SAMPLE 16
REGISTER OF MORTGAGES

REGISTER OF MORTGAGES

Register of Mortgages of ___TABLE TRAPPINGS DESIGN & MANUFACTURE INC.___

Date of Mortgage	Type of Mortgage	Short Description of Property Mortgaged	Amount of Mortgage	Name of Mortgagee or Persons Entitled to Mortgage	Where and When Registered or Filed	Date of Satisfaction Discharge or Cancellation

2. Moving Personal Assets into the Corporation

There are several ways you can go about moving your assets into your corporation.

2.1 By shareholder's loan

Let's say Mary has $5,000 of personal savings that she wants to lend to the corporation to help it cover its expenses, but she wants something from the corporation in return to protect her in case the corporation can't pay her back. She has two choices.

2.1a Promissory note

The corporation can give Mary a promissory note, a simple legal document confirming the fact that the loan was made and the corporation has promised to pay it back. The advantage of a promissory note is that it is fast and simple. The disadvantage is that it doesn't give Mary any special protection. If the corporation fails, Mary will stand in line with all the other people who are owed money. If there isn't enough to pay everyone in full, they share what's available in proportion to the amount they are owed. A sample promissory note is included here as Sample 17.

2.1b General security agreement

The other approach would be for Mary to insist that the corporation give her security for her loan over and above the simple promise to pay it back. The details of negotiating a secured loan are beyond the scope of this book, but the concept is a simple one. The corporation signs a document called a General Security Agreement that gives Mary specific rights to the equipment, machinery, and other physical assets that belong to the company. Mary must register that agreement with the Personal Property Security Registry in order to get maximum protection.

2.2 By rollover

Sally paid for a number of expensive sewing machines that she and Mary have been using to make their products. Now, Sally wants to transfer ownership of those machines to the corporation. She is free to do that, of course, but she herself may have to deal with tax consequences if this equipment had gone up in value since she bought it or if her accountant had been depreciating it while she owned it.

Such negative tax consequences would only discourage people like Sally from setting up new corporations in the first place. The government recognizes this problem, and section 85 of Canada's Income Tax Act lets

PROMISSORY NOTE

Promissory Note

For value received, Table Trappings Design & Manufacture Inc. promises to pay to the order of Mary Jones the sum of $5,000 on demand, plus interest thereon at a rate of___8___ % per annum payable before and after maturity. Notice of protest and dishonour is waived.

Dated at Edmonton, Alberta, this___10th___day of___JANUARY___, 20_01_.

Table Trappings Design & Manufacture Inc.

Sally Smith
Sally Smith, President

people transfer assets to their new corporations on a tax-free basis. This is called a rollover.

To trigger a rollover, Sally must sign a formal rollover agreement that clarifies the value of the equipment for tax purposes and sets out the price the corporation is paying for the equipment. Then that agreement must be filed with Revenue Canada. A rollover can be a complicated procedure, however, and you should always seek the help of an accountant or lawyer before attempting a rollover to your corporation.

3. Borrowing Money from a Bank

Mary and Sally could borrow money to run their unincorporated business, and their new corporation can do the same. But, as already mentioned in chapter 1, banks look at new corporations as high risk: the banks know that new corporations do not have money or other assets to secure repayment of loans. Their standard policy is to ask the individuals behind these corporations to put their personal assets on the line by signing personal guarantees.

If a corporation does have assets such as land or valuable machinery, the banks might be more relaxed about making the loan but will still ask for a mortgage on the land or a general security agreement on the machinery. To protect themselves, the banks insist that these documents be prepared and registered by a lawyer, and that the lawyer's bill be paid by the corporation. Further discussion of this issue is beyond the scope of this book, but I would advise interested readers to consult a lawyer.

4. Doing the Books

Even the smallest corporation needs the following for daily operation:

a) Its own bank account with cheques

b) A daily ledger of income and expenses

c) A filing system for invoices, bills, receipts, and all the other paper it will generate

The corporation must also reconcile the bank statement to the cash on hand every month and prepare financial statements and tax returns at the end of the year.

Mary and Sally have experience with this kind of bookkeeping, but they want to be free to focus on getting and keeping customers, so they have decided to hire a bookkeeper to look after these chores for them. They have also appointed an accountant who is familiar with small business to help them with taxes, as reflected in the minutes of the first directors' meeting.

5. Government Licenses and Regulations

5.1 Federal government

Even small corporations have to be aware of the following reporting requirements:

5.1a Goods and Services Tax

If the corporation's annual sales total more than $30,000, or if the corporation just wants to claim back the GST it pays on its supplies even though it earns less than $30,000 per year, the corporation needs its own GST number. It must also file a GST report every three months.

5.1b Canada Pension Plan and Employment Insurance

The corporation will have to deduct the appropriate amounts from the paycheques of its employees (Mary and Sally) and send them to the appropriate government departments.

5.2 Provincial government

5.2a Alberta Corporate Income Tax

Unlike other provinces, Alberta has its own office to look after collecting income tax from corporations doing business in the province. That means that Mary and Sally's corporation will have to file not one but two tax returns every year: one for the federal government and one for the Alberta government.

5.2b Workers' Compensation Board

Shortly after the certificate of incorporation is issued, Mary and Sally will get a letter from the Workers' Compensation Board asking for information about the corporation's workplace activities. They are trying to determine if this new corporation comes under the WCB's program of insurance and protection for workers who are at risk of injury.

Sally and Mary must reply, and since they intend to hire employees to make their products, they will qualify. The WCB will then determine how much the corporation has to pay. More information is available from WCB offices throughout Alberta.

5.2c Provincial licenses

Many business activities are licensed by the provincial government, including —

- real estate sales,

- securities sales,

- door-to-door and direct sales,

- franchises,

- food processing,

- transportation, and

- hotels and restaurants.

Mary and Sally's business is not one of these, so they do not have to apply for a provincial license.

5.3 Municipal regulations

5.3a Business licenses

Each municipality has the right to regulate and license the businesses operating within its territory. This includes home-based businesses that may interfere with the neighbours' enjoyment of their properties. Mary and Sally will have to check with their local municipal office to see if they need to get a business license.

5.3b Municipal taxes

Every municipality levies taxes on businesses, and on the property they own. Mary and Sally will have to contact their municipal office for details.

6. Keeping Your Corporation Alive

6.1 Annual general meeting

Once a year the corporation is required to hold a general meeting of the shareholders, and this meeting is usually followed by a meeting of the directors. Most corporations hold these meetings as close to the anniversary date of incorporation as possible.

At this meeting, the shareholders take care of the following items of business:

- re-elect directors

- ratify decisions made by directors during the past year

- dispense with appointment of auditor and appoint accountant

- review financial reports

In most cases, as we have seen, these meetings are not formally held. Instead the shareholders and directors use the provisions of By-law No. 1 allowing them to meet by phone or to waive the meeting altogether and just sign minutes that document the decisions that need to be made. Sample minutes of these annual meetings for Mary and Sally's corporation are included here as Sample 18 (Minutes of Annual General Meeting of Shareholders) and Sample 19 (Minutes of Annual Meeting of Directors).

6.2 Annual return

Every year, on the anniversary of incorporation, Corporate Registry will automatically send the corporation a document called an annual return. It is mailed to the address that the corporation gave as its registered address on the Notice of Address that was filed when the corporation was incorporated. Since this form is sent by mail, it is important that this address is kept up to date. As this is the only form that a corporation needs to file to keep its incorporated status for another year, it is important that it be filed. A corporation that fails to file an annual return for two years is automatically struck off the register by Corporate Registry. It takes time and costs money to get it re-registered.

As soon as Mary and Sally receive this form, they will fill it out (as shown in Sample 20) and take it to a private registry office for filing. Currently, the government fee for filing an annual return is $20, and the private registry will charge its own handling fee. Once the annual return is filed, Corporate Registry sends the corporation a confirmation letter that Mary and Sally will put in the corporate minute book under the tab "Annual Returns." A sample of this letter is included here as Sample 21.

7. Conclusion

Mary and Sally have successfully incorporated their own corporation under Alberta's Business Corporations Act and they are ready to move ahead with their business. Given their ambition and hard work, there is no limit to what they can achieve with their corporation.

Using this guide, you can follow their example and set up your own corporation to help you realize your business dreams.

Minutes of Annual General Meeting of Shareholders

Minutes of the Annual General Meeting of shareholders of TABLE TRAPPINGS DESIGN & , MANUFACTURE INC.

held at EDMONTON , Alberta, on the 10th day of JANUARY 20 01 .

SALLY SMITH AND MARY JONES , the shareholders of the corporation, were present and passed the following resolutions:

1) SALLY SMITH AND MARY JONES are elected directors of the corporation until further notice.

2) All things done and decisions made by the directors and officers of the corporation since the incorporation of the corporation are ratified and confirmed.

3) No auditor will be appointed and BILL ROY shall continue as accountant for the corporation.

4) The financial reports prepared by the corporation's accountant are reviewed and confirmed.

5) By signing this resolution, the shareholders waive formal notice of this meeting and ratify all business transacted.

There being no further business, the meeting was adjourned.

Sally Smith

Mary Jones

Minutes of Annual Meeting of Directors

Minutes of the Annual General Meeting of directors of___TABLE TRAPPINGS DESIGN &___,
___MANUFACTURE INC.___

held at___EDMONTON___, Alberta, on the__10th__ day of___JANUARY___ 20_01_.

___SALLY SMITH AND MARY JONES___, the directors of the corporation,
were present and passed the following resolutions:

1) ___SALLY SMITH___ was appointed President and___MARY JONES___
    Secretary Treasurer of the corporation until further notice.

2) All things done and decisions made by the officers of the corporation since incorporation are
    ratified and confirmed.

3) By signing this minute, the directors waive formal notice of the meeting and ratify all business
    transacted.

There being no further business, the meeting was adjourned.

Sally Smith
President
Mary Jones
Secretary Treasurer

Annual Return

Business Corporations Act

1. Corporate Access Number

The information contained in an annual return shall be up to date as of the last day of the anniversary month

2. Name of Corporation

TABLE TRAPPINGS DESIGN & MANUFACTURE INC.

3. Address

Address	City / Town	Province	Postal Code
9876 54 ST.,	EDMONTON	AB	A4D 5E6

4. This Report is for Year Ending _____2001_____

5. Date of Incorporation, Continuance, Amalgamation or Registration

year	month	day
2 0 0 1	0 1	1 0

6. Has there been a change of directors? ☐ Yes ☑ No

If Yes, has a Notice of Directors been filed? ☐ Yes ☐ No If No, submit with Annual Return.

7. **SHAREHOLDERS**

Name	Corporate Access Number	% of Voting Shares Issued
SALLY SMITH		
Full Address *(including postal code)*		
12345 67 AVE., EDMONTON AB A1B 2C3		50
MARY JONES		
Full Address *(including postal code)*		
12347 67 AVE., EDMONTON AB A1B 2C3		50
Name		
Full Address *(including postal code)*		
Name		
Full Address *(including postal code)*		
Name		
Full Address *(including postal code)*		

Sally Smith
Name of Person Authorizing *(please print)*

780-123-4567
Telephone Number *(Business)*

Telephone Number *(Residence)*

[DRIVER'S LICENSE #]
Identification

PRESIDENT
Title *(please print)*

2 JAN 2002
Date

This information is being collected for the purposes of corporate registry records in accordance with the Business Corporations Act. Questions about the collection of this information can be directed to the Freedom of Information and Protection of Privacy Coordinator for Alberta Registries, Research and Program Support, Box 3140, Edmonton, Alberta T5J 2G7, (780) 422-7330.

REG 3042 (99/12)

Corporate Registry

8th Floor, John E. Brownice Building
10365-97 Street
Edmonton, Alberta
Canada T5J 3W7

Telephone 403-427-2311
Fax 403-422-1091

January 10, 2002

TABLE TRAPPINGS DESIGN & MANUFACTURE INC.
9876 54 St.
Edmonton, Alberta
A4D 5E6

2002 ANNUAL PROOF OF FILING

The 2001 annual return for:

TABLE TRAPPINGS DESIGN & MANUFACTURE INC.

was filed on January 2, 2002
Payment received: $20.00

This is the only confirmation you will receive.

4
LOOKING AHEAD: BUY-SELL AGREEMENTS, UNANIMOUS SHAREHOLDER AGREEMENTS, SHAREHOLDERS' REMEDIES, AND ENDING THE CORPORATION

Mary and Sally, flushed with excitement over setting up their own corporation, are looking ahead to creating a growing and successful business. They aren't thinking about any of the difficulties that business owners often run into, such as a dispute over control or management of the corporation, or a decision by one of them to get out of the business, or the possibility that the business might fail and they might have to close down the corporation. However, any or all of these problems could come up. The following is a brief discussion of these topics, and of some steps that Mary and Sally can take now to avoid trouble later, if one of these situations does arise.

1. Buy-Sell Agreements

At this point, Mary and Sally are definitely not thinking about selling their shares and getting out of the corporation, but it could happen nonetheless for a variety of reasons, including —

- a disagreement between them about running the corporation that is so serious that one of them wants out,

- an incapacity or illness that makes it impossible for one of them to carry on,

- the death of one of them, or

- a simple decision by one of them to get out of the business and do something else.

If there are no plans in place for an orderly transfer of shares when one of these events occurs, Mary and Sally may find themselves in conflict over the price to be paid for the shares, who can purchase the shares, and where the money to purchase the shares will be found. In addition, while these issues are being sorted out, the day-to-day business of the corporation may come to a halt.

Eventually, Mary and Sally will realize it is prudent to do all they can to make satisfactory arrangements for a smooth transition if — or should I say when — one of these events comes to pass. They also realize they can best prepare for these possibilities by coming to an agreement now, when they are on good terms and the future is bright, about how they will handle the withdrawal of either of them as a shareholder.

This kind of agreement is called a buy-sell agreement. Buy-sell agreements set out the rules for shareholders to follow if one of them wants out of the corporation. They also set out rules to be followed by the executor of the estate of a deceased shareholder, should a shareholder die.

A good buy-sell agreement answers these four questions:

1) How does the agreement work?

2) When will the agreement kick in?

3) What price will be paid for the shares?

4) Where will the money come from?

1.1 How does the agreement work?

There are two common methods used to make buy-sell agreements work: the right of first refusal and the shotgun buy-sell.

The right of first refusal strategy gives the unhappy shareholder the right to offer his or her shares to the other shareholders for a fixed period of time. If the others choose not to buy them, the unhappy shareholder can sell them to anyone else who is interested when that period is over.

This approach works well from the point of view of the shareholder who wants out, but it could leave the others in a difficult spot if they can't raise the money: a total stranger could end up buying the shares. The other shareholders would then be working with someone who doesn't know them, the corporation, or its customers, which in turn could upset the smooth running of the business.

The shotgun buy-sell is designed to avoid such problems. It works like this. The unhappy shareholder gives notice of his or her desire to sell his or her shares. If the other shareholders don't buy them within a fixed time, then the unhappy shareholder automatically gets to buy the others' shares for the very same price. This means that share ownership stays among the original shareholders, resulting in the least amount of upset to the operation of the business.

1.2 When will the agreement kick in?

A buy-sell agreement should kick in whenever a shareholder is unwilling or unable to continue as a shareholder, whether during his or her lifetime or when he or she dies. The main causes that may trigger the departure of a shareholder are mentioned above, but they need not be listed in the agreement.

While it is important to have an agreement in place to cover the possibilities that can arise while the shareholders are alive, it is even more important to have one in case one of them dies. Upon the death of a shareholder, his or her shares become part of his or her estate and go to the beneficiaries of the estate. For example, in the case of Mary and Sally, Mary's shares would go to her three children, and Sally's would go to her husband, the dentist.

This could create two problems. First, Mary might not like the idea of being in business with Sally's husband any more than Sally would like the idea of being in business with Mary's kids. Second, even if the beneficiaries didn't want the shares, the surviving shareholder might be hard pressed to come up with the cash to buy them out. (This last problem is covered in section **1.4**.)

1.3 What price will be paid for the shares?

No one knows how the business of the corporation will grow, and therefore how much its shares will be worth in the future, so there is no point in setting a fixed price for shares in a buy-sell agreement. Instead, these agreements use one of three methods for setting the price when one of the shareholders wants to sell:

- The person who wants out sets what he or she thinks is a fair price when making the offer.

- A formula is given for establishing a fair price based on business factors, such as average corporate earnings, last five years' profits, or other relevant factors.

- A qualified professional, such as an appraiser, auditor, or accountant, is asked to set a fair price.

1.4 Where will the money come from?

If a shareholder wants out of a corporation, the remaining shareholders will simply have to raise the money for the purchase of the shares from the usual sources, such as borrowing from a bank. However, upon the death of a shareholder, the surviving shareholders have another option open to them: if the shareholders have had the foresight to take out life insurance policies on each other, that money can be used to purchase the shares of the deceased from his or her estate.

Let's say that Mary and Sally take out life insurance policies on each other, and each pays the premium on the other every year. When one of them dies, the money will be paid to the survivor, who will then use it to buy the shares of the deceased from her estate. There are several variations on this theme that involve the corporation paying some or all of the premiums, and there are a number of tax pitfalls of which Mary and Sally must be aware before deciding which variation is best for them. They should be sure to talk to a lawyer or accountant before proceeding.

1.5 Always get good advice

This is a simplified discussion of a complex subject. There are many pitfalls to consider when creating a buy-sell agreement, including income-tax pitfalls such as the capital-gains consequences of buying and selling shares and of using life insurance to fund the buy-out at death. A full treatment of these topics is outside the scope of this book. Consult a good lawyer or accountant before entering into a buy-sell agreement.

The sample buy-sell agreement, included here as Sample 22, contains both the shotgun and right of first refusal clauses.

2. Unanimous Shareholder Agreements

You will recall from chapter 3 that Bylaw 1 deals with the matter of a casting vote, an extra vote that can be used to break a tie. A casting vote is given to the chair of both the directors' and shareholders' meetings, and under Bylaw 1, the president of the corporation is always the chairperson of those meetings. You will also recall that at the organizational meeting of the first directors of Table Trappings Design & Manufacture

Buy-Sell Agreement

BUY-SELL AGREEMENT made the_____ day of_____, 20_____,

between___**SALLY SMITH**_____
(name)

of the city of_____**EDMONTON**_____ in the province of_____**ALBERTA**_____

(herein called_____),

and_____**MARY JONES**_____
(name)

of the city of_____**EDMONTON**_____ in the province of_____**ALBERTA**_____

(herein called_____)

WHEREAS:

(1)   The parties own or control all the issued and outstanding shares in_____

TABLE TRAPPINGS DESIGN & MANUFACTURE INC._____

(herein called "the Corporation") as follows: *(set out shareholdings)*

    SALLY SMITH — 100 SHARES
    MARY JONES — 100 SHARES

(2)   The parties desire to provide for their mutual protection if either dies or wishes to withdraw from the Corporation.

THIS AGREEMENT WITNESSES that the parties covenant and agree as follows:

1.   The parties shall not transfer, encumber, or in any way deal with any of their shares in the Corporation except as provided for in this agreement.

During the lifetime of the parties

2.   If either____**SALLY SMITH**_____ or____**MARY JONES**_____ wishes to dispose of his/her shares in the Corporation, he/she (herein called the "Offeror") shall first offer in writing to sell all his/her shares to the other party (herein called the "Offeree") on the following terms and conditions.

SELF-COUNSEL PRESS – BUY-SELL (1-1)00

3.   The offer shall contain:

(a)   an offer to sell all the shares of the Corporation owned or controlled by the Offeror (herein called "all his/her shares" or "the shares") at the arbitrary price stipulated in the offer;

(b)   an offer to purchase all the shares of the Corporation owned or controlled by the Offeree (herein called "all his/her shares" or "the shares") at the same price;

(c)   an undertaking to close the purchase or sale on a date fixed not less than ____[EIGHTY (80)]____ days and not more than____[ONE HUNDRED (100)]____ days from the service of the offer on the Offeree at the time and place fixed in the offer.

4.   If the Offeree accepts the offer to sell under paragraph 3, the Offeror (herein called "the Vendor") shall sell and transfer all his/her shares to the Offeree (herein called "the Purchaser") who shall purchase and pay for them on the date and at the place stated in the offer for the arbitrary price stipulated in the offer.

5.   If the Offeree accepts the offer to purchase under paragraph 3(b), the Offeree (herein called "the Vendor") shall sell all his/her shares to the Offeror (herein called "the Purchaser") who shall purchase and pay for them on the date and at the place stated in the offer for the arbitrary price stipulated in the offer.

6.   If the Offeree does not accept either of the alternative offers in accordance with the provisions, he/she shall be deemed to have accepted the Offeror's offer to sell all his/her shares to the Offeree and the Offeree (herein called "the Purchaser") shall purchase and pay for them on the date and at the place stated in the offer for the arbitrary price stipulated in the offer.

7.   At the time set for closing, the Vendor shall deliver to the Purchaser in exchange for the items set out in paragraph 8:

(a)   certificates for all his/her shares duly endorsed in blank for transfer;

(b)   his/her resignation from the board and that of his/her spouse and nominees, if applicable;

(c)   his/her resignation as an employee and that of his/her spouse and members of his/her family who may be in the employ of the Corporation;

(d)   an assignment to the Purchaser of all debts, if any, owing by the Corporation to the Vendor;

SELF-COUNSEL PRESS – BUY-SELL (1-2)00

(e)   a release of all claims the Vendor has or may have against the Corporation and the Purchaser;

(f)   assignment of all insurance policies on the life of the Purchaser as set out in Appendix A;

(g)   a certified cheque payable to the Purchaser for an amount equal to the aggregate of the cash surrender value of all policies on the life of the Vendor as set out in Appendix A;

(h)   all other documents necessary or desirable in order to carry out the true intent of this agreement.

8.   At the time set for closing, the Purchaser shall deliver to the Vendor in exchange for the items set out in paragraph 7 above:

(a)   a certified cheque payable to the Vendor for the full amount of the arbitrary purchase price of the shares;

(b)   a certified cheque payable to the Vendor for the full amount of any indebtedness owing by the Corporation to the Vendor as recorded on the books of the Corporation and verified by the Corporation's accountant;

(c)   a certified cheque payable to the Vendor for an amount equal to the aggregate of the cash surrender value of all policies on the life of the Purchaser as set out in Appendix A;

(d)   a release by the Corporation of all debts, if any, owing by the Vendor to the Corporation;

(e)   a release of all claims the Corporation and the Purchaser have or may have against the Vendor;

(f)   a release of all guarantees given by the Vendor on behalf of the Corporation;

(g)   all securities, free and clear of all claims, which belong to the Vendor and are lodged with any person (including the Corporation's banks) to secure an indebtedness or credit of the Corporation;

(h)   assignments of all insurance policies on the life of the Vendor as set out in Appendix A;

(i)   all other documents necessary or desirable in order to carry out the true intent of this agreement.

SELF-COUNSEL PRESS – BUY-SELL (1-3)00

9.   If on the closing date the Vendor neglects or refuses to complete the transaction or does not comply with the procedures herein set out, the Purchaser has the right upon such default (without prejudice to any other rights that he/she may have), upon payment by him/her of the purchase price (plus or minus any adjustments herein provided) to the credit of the Vendor in any chartered bank in the city of_____EDMONTON_____ (or to the solicitor for the Corporation in trust for, on behalf of, and in the name of the Vendor), to complete the transaction as above. The Vendor hereby irrevocably constitutes the Purchaser his/her true and lawful attorney to complete the said transaction and execute on behalf of the Vendor every document necessary or desirable in that behalf. [If there is more than one vendor, this power of attorney shall apply to both vendors.]

10.   If on the closing date the Purchaser neglects or refuses to complete the transaction, or does not comply with the procedures herein set out, the Vendor has the right upon such default (without prejudice to any other rights that he/she may have) to give to the Purchaser, within ten (10) days after such default, notice that on the twenty-first day after the original closing date, he/she (herein called "the New Purchaser") will purchase from the Purchaser (herein called "the New Vendor") all the shares of the Corporation owned or controlled by the New Vendor, for an amount equal to seventy-five percent (75%) of the purchase price set out in paragraph 8(a) and at the same time fix a new date within thirty (30) days and a time and place for closing; whereupon, on the new date for closing, the New Vendor shall sell all his/her shares to the New Purchaser who shall purchase the same for the new purchase price, and it is expressly agreed that all the terms of this agreement applicable to the closing of the sale and purchase of shares and to the adjustment of purchase price, if any, shall be applicable to the said closing. The New Vendor hereby constitutes the New Purchaser his/her true and lawful attorney to complete the said transaction and execute on behalf of the New Vendor every document necessary or desirable in that behalf. [If there is more than one vendor, this power of attorney shall apply to both vendors.]

11.   No offer hereunder shall be given while another offer is outstanding or a sale pending or until___[THIRTY (30)]_____ days after any sale is aborted.

After the death of a party

12.   Within___[ONE HUNDRED (100)]___ days of the death of either_SALLY SMITH_ or _____MARY JONES_____ (provided the survivor is alive on the thirtieth day after the death of the first deceased), the survivor (Purchaser) shall purchase and the estate of the deceased (Vendor) shall sell to the survivor all his/her shares owned or controlled by the deceased at the time of his/her death for the most recent price stipulated in the offer.

13. The legal representatives of the deceased shall fix, in writing, a date not more than ___[ONE HUNDRED (100)]___ days from the date of death, a time and a place for the closing of the sale of its shares.

14. At the time set for closing, the Purchaser shall deliver to the Vendor/Estate in exchange for the items set out in paragraph 15:

(a) a certified cheque payable to the Vendor/Estate for the full amount of the purchase price as set out in the offer;

(b) a certified cheque payable to the Vendor/Estate for the full amount of any indebtedness owing by the Corporation to the deceased;

(c) a certified cheque payable to the Vendor/Estate for the amount of the cash surrender value on all insurance policies on the life of the Purchaser listed in Appendix A;

(d) a certified cheque payable to the Vendor/Estate for the amount, if any, by which the aggregate net proceeds received by the Purchaser from the insurers in Appendix A exceeds the aggregate of (a), (b), and (c) above;

(e) a release by the Corporation and the Purchaser of all debts and other claims that they have or may have against the Vendor/Estate;

(f) a release of all guarantees given by the deceased Vendor on behalf of the Corporation;

(g) all securities, free and clear of all claims, belonging to the deceased Vendor which are lodged with any person (including the Corporation's banks) to secure any indebtedness or credit of the Corporation;

(h) all other documents necessary or desirable in order to carry out the true intent of this agreement.

15. At the time set for closing, the Vendor/Estate shall deliver to the Purchaser in exchange for the items set out in paragraph 14:

(a) certificates for all the Vendor's shares duly endorsed for transfer in blank with signature guaranteed by a bank or trust company;

(b) evidence of authority of executors to sign;

(c) succession duty release for the shares if applicable;

SELF-COUNSEL PRESS – BUY-SELL (1-5)00

(d)   resignations from the board and employment of all members of the deceased's family and nominees;

(e)   an assignment to the Purchaser of all debts, if any, owing by the Corporation to the Vendor;

(f)   a release of all claims the deceased Vendor or his/her Estate has or may have against the Corporation or the Purchaser;

(g)   an assignment to the Purchaser of all insurance policies on the life of the Purchaser listed in Appendix A;

(h)   all other documents necessary or desirable in order to carry out the true intent of this agreement.

Insurance

16.   In order to ensure that all or a substantial part of the purchase price for the shares of the deceased party will be available immediately in cash upon his/her death, each of the parties hereto has procured insurance on the other's life as set out in Appendix A. Additional policies may be taken out for the purposes of this agreement and they shall be added to Appendix A.

17.   Each of the parties hereto agrees, throughout the term of this agreement, to maintain and pay the premiums as they fall due on the life insurance policies listed in Appendix A owned by him/her.

18.   The insurers set out in Appendix A are hereby authorized and directed to give any party hereto, upon written request, all information concerning the status of the said policies.

19.   If any premium on any insurance policy is not paid within____[TWENTY (20)]____ days after its due date, the party insured shall have the right to pay such premium and be reimbursed by the owner together with interest at the rate of____[TW0 (2)]____ percent per month on the amount so paid in respect of such premium from the overdue payment until the date of reimbursement.

20.   Immediately upon the death of one of the parties hereto, the survivor shall proceed as expeditiously as possible to collect the proceeds of the policies on the deceased party, and the legal representatives of the Estate of the deceased party shall apply and expedite the application for letters of administration or letters probate, as may be required.

21.   The parties shall not assign, encumber, borrow upon, or otherwise deal with any of the insurance policies set out in Appendix A.

General

22.   The parties shall not throughout the term of this agreement and until a valid sale of the shares is completed under this agreement do or cause or permit to be done anything out of the normal course of business of the Corporation.

23.   Time shall be of the essence of this agreement and everything that relates thereto.

24.   The parties agree to execute and deliver any documents necessary or desirable to carry out the true purpose and intent of this agreement.

25.   This agreement shall be binding upon and enure to the benefit of the parties hereto and their respective heirs, executors, administrators, and assigns.

        IN WITNESS WHEREOF we have set our hands and our seals this_____ day of _____, 20_____.

SIGNED, SEALED, AND DELIVERED   )
in the presence of   )
)
____*J.M. Witness*____   )   ____*Sally Smith*____
(Witness signature)   )   *(Signature)*
)
____*U.R. Witness*____   )   ____*Mary Jones*____
(Witness signature)   )   *(Signature)*

SELF-COUNSEL PRESS – BUY-SELL (1-7)00

Appendix A
TABLE TRAPPINGS DESIGN & MANUFACTURE INC.
Buy-Sell Agreement

Life insurance policies on the life of___SALLY SMITH_____
owned by___[Mary Jones or the corporation]_____.

Insurer	Number	Amount

[Insert details]

Life insurance policies on the life of___MARY JONES_____
owned by___[Sally Smith or the corporation]_____.

Insurer	Number	Amount

[Insert details]

ALTERNATE VALUATION CLAUSES

Valuation by auditor — Book value at fixed date

The survivor and the executors or administrators of the deceased shall cause a valuation of all other shares of common and preferred stock of the Corporation to be made by the auditors of the Corporation based on the book value of the Corporation on the first day of the month immediately preceding the deceased's death. If within thirty (30) days the survivor and the executors or administrators of the deceased have not signified their approval of the valuation of the shares of the Corporation as determined by the auditors, the value of such shares shall be fixed by a board of three (3) arbitrators selected as follows: the survivor shall select one arbitrator, the executors or administrators of the deceased shall select one arbitrator, and the two so selected shall select the third arbitrator and the decision of a majority of the said arbitrators as to such valuation shall be final.

Book value — Capitalization of fixed assets

To the book value of the shares of the Corporation shall be added an amount equal to___[SIX]___ times the difference between the average net profit of the Corporation, after payment of all taxes and dividends for _[THREE]_ complete fiscal years of the Corporation immediately preceding the deceased's death, and _[TEN]_ percent of the adjusted net asset value of the Corporation as above determined at the date of the deceased's death.

Inc., Sally was appointed president. That means that even though she and Mary are equal shareholders, Sally has effective control over the affairs of the corporation through her casting vote.

There is nothing wrong with this, as long as Mary fully understands it and the two of them are working in harmony. But if they reach a point where they have a serious disagreement about the business, Mary may find herself powerless. If a buy-sell agreement is in place, she could use it to sell her shares and get out of the company. But there is another type of agreement that would neutralize Sally's power and preserve Mary's equality. This is called a unanimous shareholder agreement.

Unanimous shareholder agreements are used to protect shareholders by moving control of the corporation from the directors back down to the shareholders. They do that in many ways, depending on the needs of the individual shareholders who require them and the imaginations of the lawyers who create them. For example, unanimous shareholder agreements are used to —

- require the corporation to use only specific firms or individuals as advisors (accountants, lawyers);

- establish in advance the only people who can be elected as directors and officers;

- specify who can have signing authority on bank accounts;

- require the corporation to deal with a specified bank;

- limit the types of business the corporation can carry on;

- prevent the directors from entering into contracts with unauthorized suppliers;

- prevent the spending of money beyond pre-established limits;

- control the borrowing of money and the mortgaging of the corporation's assets;

- prevent payment of dividends beyond pre-established limits; and

- control hiring, firing, and compensation of key employees.

Mary could use a unanimous shareholder agreement to override the effect of the casting-vote provisions in Bylaw 1, and a sample agreement to that effect is included here as Sample 23. It is a technical document, and both Mary and Sally would be well advised to find a good lawyer to review it — or any other agreement — before they sign it.

AGREEMENT made this 25th day of October, 200–.

BETWEEN:

SALLY SMITH, of the City of Edmonton, in the Province of Alberta

(hereinafter "SMITH")

OF THE FIRST PART

—and—

MARY JONES, of the City of Edmonton, in the Province of Alberta

(hereinafter "JONES")

OF THE SECOND PART

—and—

TABLE TRAPPINGS DESIGN & MANUFACTURE INC., a corporation pursuant to the laws of the Province of Alberta

(hereinafter the "Corporation")

OF THE THIRD PART

WHEREAS the authorized capital of the Corporation is to be divided into an unlimited number of common shares;

AND WHEREAS Smith beneficially owns 100 shares and Jones beneficially owns 100 common shares, being all the common shares issued and outstanding;

AND WHEREAS Smith and Jones (hereinafter collectively referred to as the "SHAREHOLDERS") desire to provide for the constitution, organization, management and supervision of the Corporation, and for the disposition and succession of the common shares thereof;

NOW THEREFORE, in consideration of the mutual covenants and agreements herein contained and subject to the terms and conditions hereinafter set out, the parties hereto agree as follows:

1.00 CONSTITUTION

1.01   The Corporation shall not:

    a)   Amend its Article of Incorporation;

    b)   Make an arrangement;

    c)   Amalgamate;

    d)   Apply to a jurisdiction other than the Dominion of Canada for an instrument of continuation;

pursuant to the Alberta Business Corporations Act, except upon the unanimous consent of the Shareholder.

1.02   The Corporation shall not pass, amend, or rescind any by-law of the Corporation, except upon the unanimous consent of the Shareholders.

1.03   The Corporation shall not:

    a)   Redeem; or

    b)   Purchase for cancellation any of the Shares of the Corporation;

nor shall it sanction or approve any:

    c)   Conversion;

    d)   Surrender;

    e)   Allotment;

    f)   Transfer

of the shares of the Corporation, except upon the unanimous consent of the Shareholders, or as hereinafter provided.

2.00 DIRECTORS

2.01   The Board of Directors shall manage or supervise the management of the affairs and business of the Corporation.

2.02   The Board of Directors of the Corporation shall consist of a minimum of one and a maximum of three directors. The initial Board of Directors shall consist of three directors and shall include one nominee of Smith and one nominee of Jones. The third director shall be elected by the unanimous vote of the shareholders. The number of directors within the minimum and maximun range may be increased or decreased only upon the unanimous consent of the shareholders. If the Board is increased to four directors, then the Board shall consist of two nominees of Smith and two nominees of Jones. If the Board of Directors is increased to five directors the Board shall consist of two nominees of Smith and two nominees of Jones, and the fifth director shall be elected by the unanimous consent of the shareholders.

2.03   A quorum for the transaction of business at meetings of the Board of Directors shall consist of a majority of directors.

2.04   Except as otherwise provided in this Agreement, all questions proposed for consideration of the Board of Directors at any Board meeting shall, in the presence of a quorum, be determined by a majority of the directors in attendance; provided however, that the affirmative vote of at least one nominee director of Smith and one nominee director of Jones shall be required to decide any action of the Board of Directors.

3.00 **ISSUE OF SHARES**

3.01 **Pro Rata Offering**

a) Except as the parties shall otherwise unanimously agree in writing, no shares shall be issued by the Corporation unless, and each offering by the Corporations of shares shall be made, in accordance with paragraph 3.01.

b) Each offer shall be made to the shareholder as nearly as may be in proportion to the number of shares respectively held by them at the date of the offer.

c) Every offer shall be made in writing and shall state that a party which desires to subscribe for shares in excess of its proportion shall, in its subscription specify the number or amount, as the case may be, of shares in excess of its proportion that it desires to purchase. If a shareholder does not subscribe for its proportion, the unsubscribed shares shall be used to satisfy the subscription of the other shareholder for the shares in excess of its proportion. No shareholder shall be bound to take any shares in excess of the amount it so desires.

3.02 **Unsubscribed Shares** If all of the shares of any issue are not subscribed for within a period of 45 days after the same are offered to the parties pursuant to the provisions of paragraph 3.01, the Corporation may, during the next three months, offer and sell all or any of the shares not taken up by the parties but the price at which shares may be allotted and sold shall not be less than the subscription price offered to the parties pursuant to paragraph 3.01 and on terms more favorable than those offered to the parties.

3.03 **Additional Parties** Every issue of shares shall be subject to the condition that the subscriber thereof shall, if not a party hereto, agree to be bound by the terms of this agreement.

4.00 **DISPOSITION OF SHARES**

4.01 **Purchase Rights** If any shareholder (the "Offeror") desires or is required by law to transfer any of her shares to another person, or to sell or dispose of any share, the other shareholder (the "Offeree") shall have the prior right to purchase the shares on the terms and in accordance with the procedure contained in paragraph 4.02.

4.02 **Procedure on Transfers**

a) An Offeror shall notify the Corporation in writing of her desire or intention to transfer, sell or otherwise dispose of any share. The notice (the "Selling Notice") shall set out:

(i) the number and a brief description of each class of shares;

(ii) the price and terms of payment which the Offeror is willing to accept for the shares; and

(iii) if the Offeror has received an offer to purchase the shares, the name and address of the potential purchaser and the terms of payment and price contained in this offer.

b) The shares shall then be offered to the Offeree on the terms of payment and for the price contained in the Selling Notice, and shall remain open for acceptance ad hereinafter provided for a period of 45 days.

c) If, within that period the Offeree does not agree to purchase all of the shares offered, she shall be deemed to have refused to purchase the shares offered, and the Offeror may offer and sell all of the shares offered to any other person at the price and on the terms and conditions set out in the Selling Notice.

d) If all of the shares offered shall be accepted by the Offeree, the shares shall be sold to her for the price and on the terms contained in the Selling Notice.

4.03 **Additional Parties** Every transfer of shares shall be subject to the condition that the purchaser thereof shall, if not a party hereto, agree to be bound by the terms of this agreement.

4.04   **Release from Liability** If a sale, transfer or other disposition of shares is completed in accordance with this Article, the Offeror shall upon completion of the purchase be indemnified by the other shareholders from all liability or in respect of the Corporation whether under the provisions of this agreement or under any guarantee, indemnity or other financial assistance given in respect of the operations in the Corporation arising after the date of sale, transfer or other disposition and the purchase of the shares offered shall assume all obligations in respect thereof.

5.00   **GENERAL**

5.01   a)   This Agreement may be terminated upon:

          (i)   written notice from one of the shareholders to the other;

          (ii)   the bankruptcy or insolvency of either party;

          (iii)   the enactment of any legislation requiring the dissolution of the Corporation or rendering its continued operation illegal.

          b)   The Corporation shall thereupon be dissolved unless where termination occurs pursuant to paragraph 5.01 (a)(i), one of the shareholders agrees to purchase the shares of the other upon terms and conditions that they mutually agree.

5.02   **Assignment** The agreement is not assignable by any party except insofar as its benefit and burden pass with equity securities transferred in accordance with the agreement. This agreement shall enure to the benefit of and be binding upon the heirs, executors, administrators, successors, or any other legal representatives of the parties hereto.

5.03   **Additional Parties** Every issue and transfer of shares shall be subject to the condition that each subsciber or transferee, as the case may be, shall, if not a party hereto, agree to be bound by the terms hereof and become a party hereto by executing an agreement to be bound hereby.

5.04   **Miscellaneous**

          a)   The Shareholders shall not sell, assign, transfer, mortgage, charge, pledge or hypothecate their shares except pursuant to the terms hereof or except upon the unanimous consent of the shareholders.

          b)   In the event of any conflict between the terms of this agreement and the Articles of Incorporation and By-laws of the Corporation, the terms of this agreement shall prevail and the parties hereto shall forthwith cause such necessary alterations to be made to the Articles of Incorporation and By-laws as are required so as to resolve the conflict.

5.05   **Third Party Payments** Any arrangements made by the parties hereto with third parties and all payments to the third parties are the responsibility of the party entering into such arrangement and not of the other party.

          IN WITNESS WHEREOF the parties hereto have executed this Agreement as of the date first above mentioned.

SIGNED, SEALED and DELIVERED
in the presence of

_____

SALLY SMITH

_____

MARY JONES

_____

TABLE TRAPPINGS DESIGN &
MANUFACTURE LTD.

Per:_____

Incidentally, there is another way for Mary to protect her equality in the decision-making process — simply remove the casting vote provisions in Bylaw 1 before adopting it at the first meeting of the directors. Without those provisions, Mary and Sally would find themselves in a deadlock if they ever disagreed about the business. If they couldn't work out a satisfactory compromise, they would be left with two choices; either use the buy-sell agreement to get one of them out of the corporation or close the corporation down completely. Since closing down does not usually produce full value for the shares, they would likely prefer to use the buy-sell agreement. This scenario illustrates the wisdom of having a good buy-sell agreement in the first place.

3. Shareholders' Remedies

Fortunately, Mary is not totally at the mercy of Sally's casting vote. The law does give her protection if Sally uses her power to make fundamental changes to the structure governing the operation of the corporation. These fundamental changes are as follows:

- Change of the name

- Changes to the articles of incorporation, including type of business permitted

- Changes to the capital structure

- Changes to the rights of shareholders

- Registration of the corporation in another province

- Amalgamation with another corporation

- Sale or lease of all or most of the corporation's assets

If Sally tried to put through any of these changes without Mary's consent, the law gives Mary a powerful remedy — she can call for an appraisal of the fair value of her shares and then she can force the corporation to buy them from her at that appraised value.

In addition, there are other situations that give Mary special rights of which she should be aware. For example, Mary has the right to bring a lawsuit in the name of the company if Sally refuses to do so whenever the lawsuit can be shown to be in the interests of the company. This lawsuit is called a derivative action. Also, as a shareholder, Mary has the right to get a court order stopping Sally from doing something that would be "oppressive or prejudicial to the interests of any shareholder" or if Sally were misusing her powers to such an extent that it amounted to fraud.

Obviously, these are technical areas, and Mary should get the advice and assistance of a good lawyer before contemplating any of these steps.

4. Ending the Corporation

The last thing Mary and Sally may be thinking about at this point is ending their corporation, but they should know something about how that is done if the time comes. The technical term for ending a corporation is dissolution, though people also use the term winding up. Regardless of the language used to describe it, there are three common ways to end the life of a corporation, each of which is briefly discussed below.

4.1 Failure to file annual returns

If a corporation does not file an annual return for two years in a row, Corporate Registry automatically removes it from their list, which effectively cancels its incorporation and prevents it from carrying on business. This method is perfectly acceptable if the corporation has no assets; but if it does, those assets are frozen and can't be bought or sold. If Mary and Sally ever decide to end the business this way, they should make certain they sell off all the corporation's assets first.

4.2 Voluntary dissolution

This method involves applying to Corporate Registry for an official certificate of dissolution. It takes care of the problem of selling off assets or collecting unpaid bills because the law says that when such a certificate is issued, the corporation still has power and responsibility to look after those items, to pay its debts, and then to distribute any surplus to the shareholders.

4.3 Involuntary dissolution

Corporate Registry has the power to issue a certificate of dissolution or to apply to the court for a dissolution order if a corporation has not carried out any business for three years or has not filed any document that Corporate Registry requires for one year. This power is very rarely used, because if the corporation has no assets, it just lapses for failure to file annual returns, and if it does have assets, a shareholder or creditor is likely to be eager to take whatever steps are necessary to sell them and collect the money.

GLOSSARY

Articles of incorporation

A form used to incorporate that sets out basic information about the new corporation

Bylaw (often called the constitution of a corporation)

A set of rules that govern the internal affairs of the corporation

Company

Corporation

Corporation (also called a company)

A fictional entity authorized by law to carry on business. It is created by complying with the registration requirements of the appropriate government.

Creditor

A person who is owed money by another person or by a corporation

Director

One of a group of people elected by the shareholders to oversee the operations of the corporation

Distributing corporation

A corporation that is authorized to sell its shares to members of the public, usually through a stock exchange

Incorporation

The act of setting up a corporation and registering it with the appropriate government office

Incorporator

A person who incorporates a company by filing the necessary documents with the appropriate government office

Limited liability

A feature of corporations that protects the owners from being personally responsible for the debts of the corporation

Non-distributing corporation

A corporation that cannot sell its shares to members of the public and is limited to a maximum of 15 shareholders

Officer

One of the people appointed by the directors to manage the affairs of the corporation (e.g., as president, treasurer, or secretary)

Partnership

An unincorporated business carried on by two or more owners (called partners)

Perpetual existence

Unlike sole proprietorships or partnerships, a corporation does not cease to exist when its owners die

Proprietorship

An unincorporated business carried on by a single owner, who is called a proprietor

Separate legal entity

Unlike sole proprietorships and partnerships, in the eyes of the law a corporation exists independently of and is every bit as real as its owners

Shareholder

The owner of a corporation, who has the right to share in any profits it earns, the right to vote (which includes electing directors), and the right to share in the corporation's assets if the corporation ceases to do business

Trade name

The name by which a business is known. For example, Fred Smith may have a bookkeeping business known by the trade name Acme Accounting

OTHER TITLES IN THE
SELF-COUNSEL LEGAL SERIES

MANAGING A SUCCESSFUL BUSINESS IN CANADA

Dr. Tony Fattal, MBA, DCSC
Suggested retail price: $21.95

Once you have started a new business, you must turn your energies toward managing it for growth and success. This stage of business development comes with many concerns. How can you effectively deal with balance-sheet issues, cash planning and borrowing, and pricing? What is "ideal pricing"? Should you acquire another company?

These questions confront business owners and managers every day. How well you handle them can mean the difference between success and failure.

Managing a Successful Business in Canada addresses the key issues facing small-business management. Clearly written essays avoid jargon and drive straight to the heart of every manager's concern — how to make your business successful.

Topics include:

- Delegating but remaining in control

- Managing inventory successfully

- Bidding aggressively without losing money

- Converting from a service centre to a profit centre

- Dealing with an insolvent customer

- Collecting your accounts receivable while keeping your customers

STANDARD LEGAL FORMS & AGREEMENTS FOR CANADIAN BUSINESS

Stephen Sanderson, Editor
Suggested retail price: $18.95

- *Save money*

- *Enhance your business image*

- *Help your business run more smoothly*

This book belongs in every business in Canada. It provides a wide selection of indispensable legal forms and common business agreements ready to be copied onto company letterhead. The book features lay-flat binding, and all samples in this large-format volume are provided full size so it's easy to produce perfect copies without fussing over enlargements. Includes forms for:

- Letter styles and memorandum set-up

- New businesses

- Partnership agreements

- Hiring and dismissal

- Buying and selling

- Collections

- Credit/debit

CANADIAN LEGAL GUIDE FOR SMALL BUSINESS

Nishan Swais, LLB
Suggested retail price: $21.95

- *Serves as an indispensable legal resource for businesses*

- *Covers a wide range of everyday legal matters*

- *Features non-technical language*

As every owner of a small- to medium-sized business knows, legal questions frequently arise relating to the operation of a business. Yet it is not always practical to seek the advice of a lawyer for each and every legal matter.

This book was written to answer the general question, "What do I, as a business owner, need to know about the law in Canada?"

Written in straightforward language by a lawyer who specializes in business law, this book covers:

- Business structure and company law

- Contract and consumer law

- Dispute resolution

- Legislation affecting businesses

- Commonly used business documents

Order Form

All prices are subject to change without notice. **Books** are available in book, department, and stationery stores. **If you cannot buy the book through a store, please use this order form.**

(Please print.)

Name_____

Address_____

Charge to:　❑ Visa　　　❑ MasterCard

Account number _____

Validation Date _____

Expiry date_____

Signature_____

YES, please send me:

_____ *Managing a Successful Business in Canada*

_____ *Standard Legal Forms & Agreements for Canadian Business*

_____ *Canadian Legal Guide for Small Business*

Please add the applicable amount for **postage and handling** charges: $3.50 for one book; $4.00 for more than one.

Please add 7% GST to your order.

❑ Check here for a free catalogue.

Please send your order to the nearest location:

Self-Counsel Press
1481 Charlotte Road
North Vancouver, BC V7J 1H1

Self-Counsel Press
4 Bram Court
Brampton, ON L6W 3R6

Visit our Internet Web Site at:
www.self-counsel.com